Learning Through Action

The Handbook for a New Approach to Cross-Curricular Teaching

Learning Through Action

The Handbook for a New Approach to Cross-Curricular Teaching

Margaret Kay Annette Cotterill

Illustrations by Ray Thomas

Learning Through Action
The Handbook to a New Approach
to Cross-Curricular Teaching
LD856
ISBN 0905 114 68 X

First Published 1989
LDA, Duke Street, Wisbech, Cambs PE13 2AE, England
Printed in Great Britain by
Ebenezer Baylis & Son Ltd
The Trinity Press, Worcester, and London

ACKNOWLEDGEMENTS

Learning Through Action owes a great deal to the help and support of a large number of people.

We are indebted to the work of past students of Bulmershe College Reading, both undergraduate and post-graduate, who have, over the years, helped to develop and carry out the ideas. A great deal of credit is due to them and to the members of the successive Learning Through Action teams who have worked to create the programmes in this book.

We are also grateful to the many organizations who have helped us in a variety of ways, especially the World Wide Fund for Nature, the Commonwealth Institute and Digital Equipment Company.

We should also like to thank members of Berkshire Local Education Authority for their support and co-operation and finally the children and staff of the many Berkshire schools whose encouragement and enthusiasm in participating in the programmes has been so rewarding.

This book is dedicated to them.

ANNETTE COTTERILL

It is not easy to change traditional thinking on a subject and any innovator who wishes to do so must possess a wide variety of qualities: the vision to see the need for change, the creative ability to devise new methods, the courage to stand up to opposition, the patience to accept that innovation takes time and finally the tenacity to find the means to produce the reality from the idea.

In the world of education Annette Cotterill is such an individual. Early in her career in the theatre she saw the potential for using dramatic techniques in all branches of education and decided to change direction and to train as a teacher.

Over the next few years she put her ideas into practice and confirmed her theory that an active approach to teaching led to a high degree of motivation in children of all ages and all abilities.

Working as a lecturer in drama at Bulmershe College of Higher Education gave her the opportunity to develop her methods with the students and eventually an approach to teaching emerged which is now known as Learning Through Action.

CONTENTS

Part One Principles and preparation
INTRODUCTION

Learning Through Action is essentially a method of organizing and presenting materials in a particular way that is accessible to all teachers and effective for all children. It is a means of breaking down barriers and of building bridges between teacher and pupils so that all are investigating, sharing information, and building up between them a body of knowledge in an environment that they have created together. It is intended not to replace other approaches but to complement them and to increase the teacher's self-confidence.

Although role-play is an important element, teachers do not need drama experience in order to try out this way of teaching. Apart from possessing good communication skills, all they need is a belief in active learning across the curriculum and an openness of mind which sees education as an exciting exploration of ideas.

Learning Through Action began as a course for Honours elective B.Ed. students at Bulmershe College of Higher Education, Berkshire and was extended with the establishment of part-time, in-service courses for teachers. The enthusiasm of some of the teachers involved led to the formation of a group working in their spare time to devise programmes in which their own schools participated out of school hours.

It was clear from the reception of these programmes that more of this work, enabling a larger number of schools to benefit, would be eagerly received by teachers and so, in 1984, Learning Through Action became a full-time touring company, taking programmes to Berkshire schools throughout the school year.

Two years later, a full-time Diploma Course was validated (see Appendix). Now practising teachers may be seconded to spend a year learning and putting into practice the principles of Learning Through Action.

The interest aroused in the educational world has been considerable. Demonstrations at conferences, residences at a variety of museums and other educational establishments, work at the Commonwealth Institute with teachers from other countries, have all helped to spread the reputation of Learning Through Action.

The next stage is to make this type of work accessible to a greater number of children. Many teachers already use some of the techniques in their everyday teaching but would like to go further and plan their own Learning Through Action programmes. Some of these teachers work in schools using team teaching techniques, some have one or more colleagues who are interested in this approach, others will have to work alone, but all can use Learning Through Action to bring their teaching to life and to engender in children a feeling of excitement about what they are learning and an enthusiasm for education, in general.

The remainder of Part One of this book describes the philosophy of Learning Through Action and shows what it involves for both teachers and pupils. Part Two presents four complete programmes as examples. Each represents a different aspect of the curriculum.

WHAT IS LEARNING THROUGH ACTION?

The setting is a school hall, somewhere in Great Britain. There is an air of excitement and intense concentration. For over an hour, thirty-five primary school children are totally absorbed in what they are doing. Even the bell for break goes unnoticed.

Working in small groups of eight or nine, the children are hearing about and experiencing traditional Aboriginal life. Each group is gathered round its 'Aboriginal' leader on its own territory, which is represented by a coloured mat and by a screen painted with the group's totem animal. The children are discovering new wonders, from didjeridus to dilly-bags, and they are handling and finding uses for the fascinating artefacts that comprise the possessions of an Aboriginal family.

Many questions need to be answered: What kind of food is eaten? How is it obtained? How do you make a fire when you have no matches? The leaders encourage an exchange of information. Comparisons are made with the children's own lifestyles. One group searches for witchetty grubs to eat, another is learning a special dance or 'stamp', another is listening to a story of the Dreamtime and painting pictures, in Aboriginal style, of the group's totem animal.

As the children begin to understand some of the traditions of the Aboriginals, each group has an encounter with a non-Aboriginal Australian: a doctor, a missionary, a journalist, or a farmer. These people give their points of view and express their attitudes to the Aboriginal culture.

When all of the questions have been answered, all of the pictures painted, and all of the 'stamps' prepared, the groups gather together to participate in a celebration, or 'corroboree', at the circle of sand that is marked out by stones in the centre of the hall. As they join their territories together on the floor around the stamping ground, the mats form the Aboriginal flag: 'black for the colour of our skins, red for the blood which has been shed and for the colour of the earth, and the great yellow circle of sand represents the sun which links the people to the land'.

The fun of the corroboree is suddenly shattered. An angry mining engineer, who claims that the land belongs to a mining company, demands that the site is vacated because mining is about to start. The Aboriginals refuse to go and sit down with their land-rights banners. While this is happening, the children are taken back to their classroom by their teacher. There they will discuss what they have seen and done.

The memory of this experience will stay with the children for years. Issues raised will acquire a personal relevance. Information will be remembered because it has been understood, artefacts will become unforgettable when they have been used in their proper context. Future work on the topic will be greeted with excitement and enthusiasm. Above all, a group of people from a far-removed culture will have become the children's friends.

This is Learning Through Action.

The Elements of LEARNING THROUGH ACTION

What makes the situation just described different from normal classroom teaching?

1 The children are participating actively.
2 They are experiencing an event.
3 They are using their imagination.
4 They are working with a collection of artefacts.
5 The team leader is in role.
6 The work is taking place in a simulated setting.
7 Some of the work is in small groups.
8 The content is cross-curricular.
9 There is confrontation between people with different points of view, giving a balanced argument.
10 The team leaders are answering the children's questions, so that the work is flexible.
11 The work is providing the stimulus for further work on the topic.

Putting together these elements of a Learning Through Action programme results in an approach to teaching that is colourful, lively, personal, memorable, and exciting.

Looking at these elements in detail will:

- show how these elements are used in a Learning Through Action programme.
- show how you can try out some of the elements in your classroom teaching.
- provide you with a check-list to help you when you devise your own Learning Through Action programmes.

1 Active participation

Apart from a few minutes of introduction in the classroom, all children taking part in a Learning Through Action programme participate actively throughout. Active participation breaks the mould of just sitting and listening. It means, for example, exploring a polar bear's den; learning how to clean oil off a bird's feather; taking part in the evacuation of children from London in 1939; listening to an Aboriginal Dreamtime story while painting a picture in the style of Aboriginal bark painting; hearing about life in 1830 while trying to work out how to use some agricultural implement from the period.

2 The experience

Learning is not only about facts but also about feelings. Learning Through Action programmes are designed so that children learn what it feels like to be in someone else's shoes. For a short time, they may become part of a group of people who are being unfairly treated; through this, they learn to see other points of view. They may experience a day in the life of a group of people with a different cultural background who have another set of values and beliefs; through this, they understand that we all do not live in the same way. Going back in time teaches children how it would feel to live without modern inventions, such as cars, watches, radio, or television, and without the benefits of education and health care. Once children have undergone such experiences, they find it easier to understand the differences or similarities in the cultures or circumstances that they find around them.

Equally as important as the experience of a Learning Through Action programme, is the return to reality at the end, so that the children can look at the experience objectively. Responsibility for this lies with the team, one of whom should indicate to the children that s/he is no longer playing a role and should lead the children into a discussion of what they have experienced. By the time that the children return to their classroom, they should understand what the programme has been about and should be in a position to make rational rather than emotional judgements about what has taken place.

3 Use of imagination

The world of a child is twofold: there is the outer world which adults can see but, just below the surface, there is another world of fantasy which the child can enter and leave at will. Suspension of disbelief is a convention that children understand completely and use in their games. A skilful team member can easily persuade a group of children to crawl through an imaginary rainforest and communicate with a group of gorillas that they find there or to look through a pair of real binoculars and see an imaginary mother polar bear and her cubs emerging from their den.

There is no problem in telling a class of 8-year olds that they are going on a journey to Australia, for example. With the help of a few posters, the corridor between classroom and hall can become an airport and the hall itself is accepted as being Australia. When the programme *My Land* was presented no child ever questioned that a group of young white teachers were Australian Aboriginals. They were introduced as such, they wore land-rights tee- shirts, and they were sitting on a circle of sand on the floor of the school hall. The children understood and accepted the 'contract', reacting to them as if they had been Aboriginals in Australia and the circle of sand their sacred site.

4 Employment of artefacts

Many teachers, seeing a Learning Through Action project, will comment on the artefacts that are used. These are an important feature of a programme. Good artefacts can transport a child to another country or a different time. Focusing attention upon an interesting object encourages children to try using it and to ask questions about it. It can also provide a way in to the discussion of an issue. An ashtray made out of an elephant's foot can conjure up a picture of the elephant as it was in the wild and can lead on to a discussion about poaching and why this takes place. A didjeridu being played can bring to life another culture, through the atmosphere created by the strangeness of the music. Being allowed to try out old farm implements or Victorian kitchen equipment helps to foster the feeling of going back to past times and excites the children, who want to know more about the background and lives of the people who owned and used such things.

The management of artefacts is important, since children must be allowed to handle and touch things, in order to find out how they work. Being allowed only to look can be frustrating and can lead to loss of interest. Anything that is used, therefore, should be sturdy and unbreakable.

Obtaining artefacts is a challenge but it is surprising how many parents and friends will be able to help. There are also many organizations, such as national and local museums, which are usually willing to lend out artefacts for use in a programme directly or, in the case of something more delicate, for a copy to be made. Art and craft departments in nearby secondary schools and technical colleges may also help with construction work. Children may be asked to make their own artefacts. For example, in the programme about evacuees, all of the children make gas-masks and identity cards during a preliminary practical session.

Artefacts alone, however, are not as effective as using them in conjunction with role-play. Teachers and students have discovered that basing a history lesson on a group of artefacts stimulates children but that assuming the role of the owner of the artefacts considerably increases the children's interest and concentration.

5 Role-play

Role-playing is an extension of imagination. Children assume roles in their games which help them to learn about life and to solve their problems. However, it is not only children who are adept at this skill; all of us practise it whether or not we realize it. In the course of a day, we may play the role of wife or husband, parent, child, teacher, pupil, and many others.

A good teacher uses role-play constantly, slipping into a different role to make a point, to elicit information from children, to act as 'devil's advocate', or to tell a story. A more elaborate use of role-play is for a teacher to take on a researched role in order to make a lesson come alive. An historical event will become more exciting and more significant if the teacher assumes the role of a character from the period. Children respond well to this approach; they enjoy it, they retain information well, and they are encouraged to ask questions.

Teachers may feel that they lack the confidence to try this approach but it requires little more than the skills of good story-telling, which most teachers already possess. For example, in the programme *Animal Watch*, a teacher who was playing the role of a conservationist needed to explain the point of view of the poacher. Instead of describing this to the children, she simply put on a different hat. For a short time, she became the poacher and told his story.

A class teacher can easily use this technique without elaborate preparation. One or two simple items of costume will convey enough information to the children and their imagination will do the rest. In *My Land*, one team member assumed several different roles without using elaborate make-

up or costume. The children accepted that, when he wore an airline badge, he was a benign representative of an airline but that he became the hostile mining engineer when he put on a hard hat and overalls.

All you need to do, to try this type of role-play, is:

- to acquire sufficient background knowledge of a subject or character.
- to find one or two items of costume that will convey the character to the children.
- to be prepared to be in a vulnerable position!

Start by taking on a role of authority, so that your relationship with the children is similar to that of teacher to pupils. Once you feel confident in this type of role, ease off the authority and allow the children to be in a superior position. They will then feel that they are doing the work.

This is the first step towards Learning Through Action.

6 Simulated settings

A Learning Through Action programme is always identified with a particular setting. This setting may be a simple representation on a painted screen, giving the atmosphere of the country or environment to be visited, or more elaborate painted scenery, such as in *Animal Watch* where it depicts the savanna or the rainforest and completely encloses each working area, or simply a box of artefacts on a coloured mat, where the artefacts provide the atmosphere.

The setting is always attractive, colourful, and full of interest, and provides a defined area in which the small groups work. In some programmes, use is made of a special environment, such as a local Elizabethan manor house for an historical programme. On one occasion, for example, the team was invited to present the farming programme, *Seasons of Change*, for a week at an open-air museum in Somerset. They worked in an authentic barn containing farm implements from the last century.

The increased interest of the setting sparks the imagination of the children, helping them to progress beyond sitting and hearing about a topic to becoming a part of the action. This linking of the setting to what is being learned helps the processes of understanding and retaining information.

7 Small-group work

One of the most important features of a programme is that the main body of work is done in small groups. These consist of not more than ten children working with one team member within a defined space. Many teachers already use small-group work, dividing the class into three or more groups, setting each a task, and moving from group to group giving advice and help. The benefits gained from this kind of work can be seen even when used only occasionally.

Individual attention The usual arrangement for group work is for everyone to sit on the floor in a circle. This means that the children are constantly in eye contact with the team leader, giving each child a feeling of personal involvement and importance. Because the group is small, all members have an equal chance to try out artefacts and to practise skills. If the team members and the children are not well known to each other, all of the children should be labelled with their first names and the team with their role names, so that communication is personal and a relationship develops between the group during a programme.

Concentration Concentration is greatly helped because each child is close to the focus of attention; that focus is constantly changing, so that there is always something exciting to do or to see. Concentration is reinforced by the immediate background, which is related to the topic, making it less easy for the attention to stray.

Security Timid children feel safer by being part of a small, defined group and will relax sufficiently to join in more than usual. Because of this feeling of security, a hidden strength or ability may emerge which might otherwise go unnoticed. A child with special knowledge of a country will find it easier to share this with a small group rather than with a whole class. For example, in a programme set in India, one child revealed a

deep knowledge of and skill in Indian dance, which he shared with his group and so enriched this part of the programme. A child who has had such an experience in the safety of a small group may gain the confidence to demonstrate his/her skills to the whole class at a later date.

Opportunity In a small group there is no necessity to speak loudly, since all can hear everything that is said, and a child who is slow to react is given the chance to speak. In a mixed-ability group, children with learning difficulties are able to participate alongside the mainstream children.

Identification Belonging to a special group in a programme engenders a feeling of pride in that group. Letters from children who have taken part in a Learning Through Action programme often stress the importance to them of being part of a named family (as in *Seasons of Change*) or of belonging to a special group of Aboriginal people from a particular area of Australia (in the programme *My Land*). This feeling of belonging increases the contribution that individual children make to the programme.

Co-operation Following on from such identification is a wish for the success of the group. This brings about a special type of co-operation because all of the group members have the urge to help each other. In one special school, the groups consisted of children with varying learning difficulties. All of the children worked well together. Those with more ability were especially encouraging to children with severe difficulties, helping them to join in the activities at their own level.

Control The lack of discipline problems during programmes shows the efficacy of small-group work in combating any disruptive or bored children in a class. Teachers frequently comment on the involvement and responsiveness of a child who is habitually disinterested or unruly in class. Such a child may be unwilling to participate because of anxiety about the written aspect of school work and the consequent fear of failure. Once this threat is removed, natural curiosity and interest are aroused. The confidence gained by participation in a programme will often extend into other areas of school life.

8 Cross-curricular approach

All Learning Through Action programmes are cross-curricular and feed into the core curriculum. The content of a programme may include maths, science, English, history, geography, and biology, as well as practical activities such as art, crafts, construction work, music, dance, and drama. A programme may therefore become the stimulus for a wide variety of more intensive follow-up work on a particular subject.

9 Balanced argument

The Learning Through Action team believes that no group has the right to stamp its own philosophy upon a child or school and that a lack of a balanced argument in a programme is morally wrong. Some programmes, especially those for Infants, may need to be more didactic, particularly when dealing with such topics as healthy eating and care of the environment, but all children, no matter how young, always have the freedom to give their point of view without any fear of disapproval from the team.

One of the main aims of the programmes for Juniors is that children should learn the importance of looking at problems from someone else's point of view. Once they have had experience of this, it becomes much easier for them, in the future, to appreciate that there is always more than one side to an argument. In the programme *Animal Watch*, environmentalists, conservationists, and zoo-keepers are all represented. The children are encouraged to listen to all views before saying what they themselves think.

In a programme about the Arctic, a British zoologist is shocked at the killing of seals. The indigenous people explain to her/him the difference between subsistence hunting, which is hunting for necessary food, and the hunting of animals for pleasure or for the profit to be made from the sale of skins. The children are able to learn that what may appear wrong by one set of standards could be seen quite differently by people from another part of the world and with a different culture. This type of programme is therefore at the heart of multi-cultural education.

10 Flexibility

Since Learning Through Action programmes are unscripted and since all groups of children have different abilities and interests, much flexibility is needed by team members. Flexibility within a programme means knowing what are the needs of the children at any particular moment: when to be close to the children and when to stand apart from them; how far to take an argument; when to talk and when to listen; when to use a pause to effect and when to jump in with a remark; when to be serious and when to use humour. This necessitates a thorough knowledge of the subject, an open mind that is willing to pursue new ideas, and the ability never to allow the performance of a role to take over from the child-orientation of a programme. Sometimes this means taking the lead from the children when an interesting point is raised. The Learning Through Action team member/teacher never threatens, never lectures, never scoffs, never dampens enthusiasm and, above all, never speaks down to a child nor attempts to demonstrate superiority.

Flexibility comes with practice but must be a feature of all programmes so that each one is fresh and unique to a particular group of children on a particular day. Although the basic outline remains the same, a programme should always be developing new aspects and should never be the dull repetition of a formula.

11 Follow-up work

From the earliest days of Learning Through Action, a programme has always been intended to be not an isolated event but a stimulus to further work on the topic, which will be carried out by the class teacher. Over the years, it has been noted that a topic that is started by a programme produces feelings of excitement and involvement in children which will continue for weeks afterwards. The experience which they have had makes follow-up work personal and special and it is enthusiastically undertaken.

HOW CAN I START ROLE-PLAY WITH MY CLASS?

Decide which project would lend itself to role-play. (An historical subject may be easiest to start with.)

TO PLAN YOUR ROLE

Think about what sort of person you might be.

Make a note of:–

YOUR NAME
YOUR OCCUPATION
YOUR AGE
THE YEAR
FAMILY DETAILS
WHERE YOU LIVE
WHAT YOUR HOUSE IS LIKE
WHAT SORT OF LIFE STYLE YOU HAVE
WHO YOUR NEIGHBOURS ARE
WHAT WORK YOU DO OUT OF THE HOME
HOW TO USE THE ARTEFACTS YOU ARE SHOWING
WHETHER YOU EARN ENOUGH TO KEEP YOURSELF AND FAMILY
WHAT SORT OF SITUATIONS YOU MIGHT FIND YOURSELF IN
HOW YOU MIGHT REACT TO THESE SITUATIONS
WHAT SORT OF FEELINGS YOU MIGHT HAVE
ETC. ETC.

This should give you enough to answer many of the children's questions.

Pick out one or two artefacts to show to the children. (These may have been lent by friends or borrowed from a local museum, etc.)

Decide who might have used these artefacts.
Read up the historical background as if you were planning a lesson.

Decide:
- what clothes you will need to suggest the character.
- what events you will talk about.
- what issues you will raise.

To do a planned role-play
Set out your artefacts in the classroom.

Either leave the room for a minute and come back in costume or put on your costume in the classroom.

Start to talk to the children in your role.
Encourage the children to question you about the artefacts and your role.
If you do not know the answer to a question, improvise but do not come out of role.

At the end of the role-play
Take off an item of clothing, such as a hat, indicating to the children that you are no longer in role. (This is known as *'de-roling'.*)
Discuss the role-play with the children.
Tell the children if there were questions that you could not answer. Ask them how they could find out the answers for you.

The children will soon get used to this approach and will look forward to meeting new characters.

On some occasions you may find that you can use role-play spontaneously to help to describe an artefact.
Encourage the children to try role-play to describe artefacts, which they have brought to school, to the rest of the class.
Start a hat box, asking for contributions from children, parents, and friends. This will provide a source of costume for children wishing to adopt a role.

Can any teacher use Learning Through Action?

Over the last ten years, Learning Through Action has become well known in Berkshire schools through the touring of the Learning Through Action team. There are now also many teachers who have had experience of using this approach to teaching, either as students at Bulmershe College, Reading, or by taking the Learning Through Action Diploma course at the Learning Through Action Centre. These teachers are now planning programmes in their own schools and are finding them highly successful.

A new topic may be introduced by putting aside a whole week during which a Learning Through Action programme that is planned by a group of teachers will be presented to every class in the school. Those teachers who want to be involved become part of the team, while others may help with research, with finding or making artefacts, with making costumes, or by taking duties for the teachers involved.

A typical example took place recently at a school in Reading. One of the teachers there had been introduced to Learning Through Action through an in-service course and had worked on several programmes since then. Another took the diploma in Learning Through Action in 1987-88. Seven teachers in the school agreed to take part, the rest being willing to take on extra numbers in their classes during the week of presentation of the programme.

The topic concerned the threat to a local community posed by the proposed development of a leisure complex which would lead to major environmental changes in the area.

The team members undertook to research their own characters and to find their costume. Together they planned the details of the programme, including the roles and any necessary dialogue.

Some time was put aside to plan artefacts and equipment and to rehearse the roles, the group work, and the dialogue.

The programme took about 1½ hours for each group of 35-40 children. During the week, all 350 pupils in the school participated. It was an enjoyable and useful exercise, not only as an exciting introduction to the subject of the environment but also as a means of uniting the whole school in one project.

In several other schools, ex-diploma students have planned similar programmes with great success. However, there is no reason why those who have never seen a Learning Through Action programme should not start by reading about the principles of the method and then trying out some of the programmes that are described later in this book.

Which Children can participate in Learning Through Action?

Learning Through Action is suitable for any age group, including young adults with special needs. The programmes that are described later in this book are especially designed for 7-12 year olds but may be used with younger children or older students. The Learning Through Action team has also presented many secondary programmes, which, although they follow a slightly different format, are based on the same principles.

Because of the flexible nature of the work, it is possible to adapt a programme to a range of age groups. If working with a succession of classes, the team can adjust the programme to the level of understanding of a particular group. In many small, rural primary schools, which are visited by the Learning Through Action team, the whole school will take part in one programme. The older children help the younger, and teachers say that the children benefit from working together as a group. All will participate at their own level and the follow-up work will be of interest to the entire school. This work is therefore ideal for the small school.

Children with special needs and mixed-ability groups

Although most children with severe learning difficulties attend special schools or units, there is a growing trend towards the integration of children with moderate learning difficulties into the mainstream. When watching a mixed-ability group involved in a Learning Through Action programme, it is almost impossible to tell which children are those with special needs. This is because this type of work draws on their personal resources and practical abilities rather than requiring them to demonstrate any particular literacy or numeracy skills. Material is adapted so that children with varying cognitive and literacy levels can understand equally. The informality and flexibility provide a relaxed atmosphere which brings out the best in all children. The more able gain confidence by helping the less able and the less able learn a great deal from the example of the others.

One such group consisted of children with varying degrees of learning difficulty, from moderate to severe. The children were exploring a box of Indian artefacts and planned to act out an episode from the story of Ramayana. They went to great lengths to ensure that a boy with cerebral palsy and consequent walking difficulty was able to take part. Helping the boy not only gave a great deal of pleasure to the boy himself but also increased their confidence and sense of responsibility.

At the same school, one group included an autistic boy who chose to sit apart from the rest of the children while the team leader told a folk story with mimed actions. All of the other children joined in the actions but this boy was apparently quite unaware of them. As the story proceeded, however, his attention was caught by a particular action and, although limited in his co-ordination, he managed to copy the team leader. The other children, noticing this, moved to make room for him in the circle and encouraged him to join them. Finally he began to attempt to articulate some of the words of the story. For the rest of the morning, this boy experienced working as part of a group and integrating with other children.

The Learning Through Action team has also demonstrated that, by adapting material that is used for mainstream groups, it is possible to work with both children and adults with severe learning difficulties. The team was invited to present a programme on good eating habits at a special school. The programme had been designed for Infants but would, in this case, be presented to one group of 12-16 year olds and to another group aged between 16 and 19 years, in the extended education unit. A teacher from the school saw the programme beforehand and suggested some minor adjustments. Because of the difficulty for these students of understanding the basic concept of the programme (the 'traffic lights' system of identification of food values), this idea was first introduced by the class teachers, so that it was familiar to the students by the time of the team's presentation. Since concentration is limited for these students, an opening slide sequence was reduced in length. The chorus of a song, which is normally taught during the programme, was learned before the day of the programme. The team members spoke very slowly and were sensitive to the fact that, although the learning age was much lower, the actual age was 12-19 years.

The success of the morning session was described by the teacher who had arranged the visit. 'For at least an hour and a quarter, the team held the attention of all thirty students. I made a point of looking at each face. Some of our students' ability to concentrate is extremely limited; they have to be constantly encouraged to listen and are easily distracted. All faces bore expressions of rapt attention, hands were shooting up eagerly, and answers were being given to questions asked by the team. Each individual got an opportunity to participate and be heard.'

The benefit to children with physical disabilities is equally noticeable. Children who are confined to wheel chairs are able to experience a release of their feelings of frustration by taking on different roles. The result of a programme in one school was a request from the pupils for more of this type of teaching, which, they felt, was especially important for them. A former team member, who now works in a school for children with physical and/or learning problems, finds that, where the individual needs of his students overlap, it is very successful to work with the resulting small groups on projects that are based on the principles of Learning Through Action.

What special skills are taught by Learning Through Action?

Listening

The first stage in learning is the ability to listen. Many children come to school without this basic skill. They have often spent many hours sitting in front of bright images on a television screen, which requires them to make little effort and they soon forget what they have heard. Listening therefore, is a skill that needs to be taught.

Teachers often say that one important aspect of the Learning Through Action method is the dramatic surprise element that plunges the children into a new situation which they do not quite understand. The result is that they must listen carefully in order to find out what is happening and how they should proceed. They soon become so involved in the action that they begin to listen and participate rather than merely hearing passively.

Language Development

The learning of communication skills is at the heart of education. Learning Through Action aims at giving children the understanding, confidence, imagination, and sensitivity that will help them to become fluent in speech and therefore good communicators. The long-term result of this is an enthusiasm for learning which will set them on the path to self-education.

The process of language development is tackled in several ways within a programme:

New vocabulary Every programme involves the child in an experience that takes place in different surroundings (the simulated setting). This transportation immediately presents the child with the need to acquire a special set of words and expressions in order to cope with the new environment. In the programme *Animal Watch,* words such as *Habitat* and *Extinction* and phrases such as *Endangered species* are introduced by the team leader, who explains them in simple terms to the children. Throughout the programme, the children are encouraged to use the new expressions, which rapidly become part of their everyday vocabulary. Another example of this is the acquisition of new words in connection with a new activity. In learning the threshing process in *Seasons of Change*, a whole set of words, such as *Flailing*, *Winnowing*, *Chaff*, is also learned. These words become part of a child's latent store of specialized vocabulary, to be called upon when necessary.

Reporting skills At some point during a programme, the information that is acquired in small-group work is always shared with members of other groups. In *Animal Watch*, five groups of children are allocated to different habitats, where they find out about the animals living there. At the end of this part of the programme, the children in each group are asked to report back to the rest of the class what they have learned. This gives the children not only practice in the art of reporting but also confidence in speaking to the whole class as experts on a subject. An extension to this ability is the practice that is acquired in answering questions which are posed by the rest of the group.

Reasoning skills The development of these is linked to the learning of assessment and decision-making skills. In *Animal Watch*, for example, the 'design' groups are expected to argue with controversial characters who try to impose their ideas on them. When children feel strongly about a situation, they often find themselves able to draw on latent reserves of language in order to put their case to someone with whom they disagree.

Questioning and choice of language A programme is designed not only for the imparting of knowledge but also for the exchange of information and ideas. In the programme *My Land*, the children go on a journey to find out about the Aboriginal people of Australia but the Aborigines also ask the children about their own lives and customs. Thus the children must learn how to formulate questions in order to elicit information and also to answer questions in a way that is understandable by people who may know little about their way of life.

A situation might arise in which children need to explain everyday objects and events to someone with whom they have few common terms of reference. They are then put in the position of having to use language with great care and precision. In programmes where children are working 'in role', they will often produce a greater variety of language in their questions and responses than they would normally employ.

Removal of pressure and expectations A class teacher will often remark that a child who has contributed enthusiastically during a programme is one who rarely speaks as a rule. It is clear that the informality of the situation inspires children who are shy about talking in class. Being in a supportive atmosphere gives them the confidence to put their thoughts and feelings into words. Children with reading and writing difficulties often express themselves well orally in a situation where the former skills are temporarily not required.

The confidence that is gained from participating in a programme often has long-lasting effects in language development. The excitement that is engendered by the experience may inspire children to wish to communicate their feelings to the rest of the school. This can result in further extending the use of the spoken word by presenting an assembly which is inspired by the programme. Increased confidence may also extend into written work. Children who have writing difficulties often feel inspired to write creatively after participating in a programme.

Evaluation and Decision Making

Every programme places children in situations where they are required to combine an experience with the assimilation and evaluation of facts, in order to make choices and decisions. In

Seasons of Change, the children are asked to decide, having taken into account their family circumstances and the opinions of other people in the village, whether they wish to demonstrate against the introduction of agricultural machinery. In *Animal Watch*, they learn about the needs of animals by 'visiting' different habitats and then formally debating the relative merits of several schemes that are designed by themselves to benefit animals. There is never any indication of a 'right' or a 'wrong' answer but all children are encouraged to put their own views without pressure. A frank expression of ideas is helped by the fact that, during many programmes, the children are working 'in role' as researchers or reporters and as such can relate the decisions which are made to the situation which they are experiencing.

How else do children benefit?

Retention of information

When teachers are asked about ways in which they think that this method of teaching affects children's ability to learn and retain information, they will give many different answers. Some feel that it is the role-play that is the important factor; some talk of the impact of working with adults who, during a programme, treat the children as equals; some stress the aid to memory of linking information to artefacts; others feel that the children, because they are allowed to initiate areas of discussion, remember what they are told more clearly. All, however, agree that the ancient maxim of 'I do, I understand' is at the root of the successful retention rate which is always noted. Many teachers find that, even as much as two years after a programme, the majority of children remember the work and their feelings about it in great detail.

Motivation

One important result of Learning Through Action programmes, which are highly concentrated and which involve the children completely, is the motivation that they produce. Teachers find that children go home from school still discussing what they have experienced in a programme; parents notice that they talk about it at home and are keen to take in any relevant artefacts that they may have. They return to school eager to know more about the different environment that they have 'visited' and the characters whom they have met. Follow-up work and meaningful research on the topic is undertaken with a high degree of interest and enthusiasm.

It is often the children who are normally least motivated who contribute to a programme. These children thrive in an environment in which there is no pressure, and no time for boredom, but instead there is a great deal of action and 'hands on' experience, as well as the need for responsibility and decisiveness.

Integration

These programmes can help to create links with the rest of the school, in the form of assemblies, exhibitions, and special events for the entire school, which are based on the topic.

Links can also be made with the home and the community, especially through local history and environmental programmes. The interest that is aroused at home can result in feedback from parents, grandparents, and other older people, thus encouraging them to feel involved in their local school.

For instance, after the programme *The Evacuees*, many grandparents in the Reading area, who had been involved in the evacuation during the Second World War, contributed to the follow-up work, either by sending memorabilia to exhibit or by coming into school to talk about their own memories.

In addition, there are links with other schools, which foster a feeling of community and common purpose. Groups of schools in the same area can collaborate in the preparation of programmes in which teachers and children from the different schools take part.

For example, the response to the programme *My Land*, which was presented in several schools by the Learning Through Action team, was so great, and so much interesting follow-up work was sent to the group, that it was decided to organize a special follow-up event. This took the form of a festival or 'Corroboree' to which all schools who had participated in the programme were invited.

A large school hall was acquired and each participating school prepared an individual 5-minute event which was inspired by the topic. These varied from music and dance to enactments of stories or ideas which they had researched for themselves. Interspersed with the school contributions were new items from the team in the form of songs and dances, in which the children were encouraged to join. Schools that did not wish to participate sent follow-up work, which resulted in an extensive and varied exhibition that was displayed on the same occasion.

The outcome was a feeling of common interest and friendliness between the schools involved.

How do I begin to plan a programme?

You have tried out some role-play and now feel ready to tackle a Learning Through Action programme. Where do you begin?

You can start either by using one of the programmes that are described in this book or by planning your own programme on a topic of your choice.

If you have to work on your own, it is advisable to use the lesson plans that are described at the end of the programmes. These will cover the same ground as a programme but will extend over several lessons.

To plan your own programme, you must:

1 Choose a *Topic*.
2 Define your *Aims*.
3 Decide on the *Objectives*.
4 Start *Research*.
5 Write an *Outline scenario*.
6 Decide on *Roles*.
7 Plan the *Programme* in detail.
8 Work out *Practical organization*.

1 Topic

Learning Through Action techniques can be applied to any topic or subject.
The topic itself is only a starting point, as programmes are cross-curricular. One programme may include a wide range of core curriculum subjects such as English, history, geography, maths, and science, as well as art and craft, music, drama, and dance.

Over the last few years, some of the areas that have been explored have been as follows.

Specific historical periods Experiencing events from the past can help children to understand contemporary issues. The programme *Seasons Of Change* will give children an historical insight so that follow-up work, such as looking at change and progress in this century, will acquire a new relevance.

Local history Finding out about past events in the local community helps children to identify with that community. Such programmes can forge valuable links between children and other family members by means of memories or stories that have been handed down. *The Evacuees* prompted a great deal of interest from Reading people who, in response to a local radio programme, contributed to an exhibition about the

Second World War and the evacuation which was arranged by Learning Through Action.

Geography A topic such as the building of a new town can introduce ideas of land use, town planning, housing, employment, and change, as well as developing a sense of social responsibility.

Science A programme about a subject such as industrial chemical pollution includes specific scientific information as well as discussion of the effects of such pollution on people and the environment.

Maths A programme about the setting up of a fête is used to teach practical maths, including basic arithmetic, fractions, areas, co-ordinates, etc.

Different cultures Exploring other ways of living provides a way in to such issues as the effect of change and progress, care of the land, and multi-cultural studies. *My Land* is only one of a series which includes *The Yanomami Indians of Brazil*, *The Inuit of Canada*, and *Islands at Sea* (a programme about the Pacific Islands).

The environment Conservation and care of the environment are major concerns today. These issues may be the topic for a complete programme as well as an important part of the content of other programmes. *Animal Watch* deals with the destruction of habitats, which can lead to the endangerment and/or extinction of species.

Social issues Programmes about such problems as homelessness encourage children to face up to their social responsibilities. They also help them to learn about problem solving, choices, and decision making.

Personal development Older pupils have the opportunity to find out about some of the life skills that are needed both during and after leaving school, such as dealing with peer pressures, exploring information technology, or starting up a small business.

Tips

Choose a topic that you will all enjoy working on.
Give yourselves some time to think over the topic and do some background reading before embarking on any planning.
Bear in mind any special skills or strengths that your team members may have.

2 Aims

The overall aim of a programme is what you hope to achieve by it.

3 Objectives

These include:

- what you want the children to learn.
- what you want them to experience.
- what skills they will acquire.
- which issues should be discussed.
- links which can be made between the programme and the children's experience of life.

4 Research

Try to find personal contacts who will be able to give first-hand or specialized information. Talk to as many people as possible in order to ensure that facts are correct.

Use:

- libraries
- library archives
- magazines
- videos
- slides
- museums
- conservation organizations
- specialist organizations

The first stage is to do some general background reading in order to obtain ideas for the story-line.

Once the outline has been planned, research more fully the areas that you will be including in the programme.

Remember that the children will be asking questions, so make sure that your research is thorough.

5 Outline scenario

A scenario is the planned structure of a programme: how to begin, how to end, and what happens in between. It includes the story-line, the characters, the dialogue, and the settings.

At this stage, plan an outline scenario, which is the basic idea, and fill in the details later.

6 Roles

Decide what roles will be needed.
Decide who will play which roles, according to the number in the team.

7 The programme in detail

When you are planning a programme:

- plan each section in turn.
- keep the aims in mind.
- keep the objectives in mind.
- remember the elements of Learning Through Action.

The beginning

The initial encounter must be carefully planned. The degree to which this wins the confidence of the children and arouses their attention and interest will determine the success of the whole programme.

Consider:

- who will do the introduction.
  The first contact should be made by one person; meeting a whole team at once is confusing or intimidating, especially for younger children. The choice of role may be one of authority but it should be someone who will reassure the children and who has the enthusiasm to stimulate them and arouse their curiosity.

- where the introduction should take place.
  The first contact should be made in the classroom, as it is best to start in familiar surroundings.

- how to meet the children.
  Experience has shown that it is more successful for the team member to be in role from the start. The children then feel immediately involved and understand that they must enter into a 'dramatic contract'. The element of surprise adds an extra dimension.

- the way in.
  The early part of a programme must include some element which not only arouses the curiosity of the children but also coincides with their experience of life. They need to start from a point which is familiar and with which they can identify.

- the impact.
  The start should also include something that makes a strong impression on the children. Dramatic impact produces a feeling of excitement and helps them to remember what they have learned.

The opening section should take no more than fifteen minutes.

The main body

This may be divided into spells of small-group work, large-group work, and sometimes individual work.

Small-group work

One team member works in a defined space with not more than fifteen children.

The content of the small-group work consists of:

- information exchange between the team leader and the children.
- practical work arising from this.

● skills such as art, crafts, construction work.
● discussion of issues arising from the situation.
● exploring, handling, and use of artefacts.
● music, drama, dance, and story-telling.

This part of the programme should be flexible and the detail of the content should be tailored to fit the interest and abilities of the particular group.

Large-group work.
While small-group work forms the major part of a programme, some activities require the whole group to work together. This may be in order that the children can share with each other what they have been doing in their small groups, or can discuss issues, or can take part in larger-scale activity such as a forum or meeting, a debate, a trial, or a social event.

The ending
Make sure that by the end of the programme the whole group knows what has been happening in other groups.
Remember that children may end up with strong feelings about a situation which they have experienced. It is important, therefore, that they have a short time in which to calm down and become more objective about their experiences. At the end of a programme, one member of the team should stop playing a role and should talk to the children as her/himself. This 'de-roling' is achieved by the team member, for example, taking off one or more items of costume. From this the children understand that they too should drop any role of researcher, reporter, or detective which they may have taken on and should join in the discussion as themselves.

8 Practical organization

Set a date, well in advance (Immediately after half-term will give time for organization and last-minute arrangements.)
Book the hall.
Alert the rest of the school.
Organize:

● costume.
Most teachers will be able to find one or two suitable items of costume. Use drama wardrobes or ask friends for special items.

● settings
If these need painting, either enlist the help of the art department in a nearby school or have the children do it in a preliminary session.

● artefacts, materials, and equipment.
Make a detailed list of: — what is available at school.
—what needs to be found or collected.

—what you may have to buy (if you have a budget).
—what you can borrow.
—what you or other team members or other colleagues can make.
—what the children can make.
Plan when these will be made or produced.

- preliminary work with children.
  Organize one or more practical sessions during which the children can make settings or artefacts.
  Do not reveal what will take place in the programme. This is most important.

- a rehearsal schedule.
  This need not take up much time but is necessary so that problems are solved beforehand.

Rehearse:

- roles.
  Build a character as suggested in the section on role-play. Try out the role with the other members of the team.

- dialogue.
  Some set dialogue may be needed between the characters in order to further the action in the programme.

- small-group work.
  Plan what practical work you will include, what information you will give, what issues you will discuss, etc. Try out the work using the other members of the team as the 'children' in your group.

- management of artefacts.
  Learn how to use anything unfamiliar, so that you can easily teach the children.

- setting up of hall.
  Plan how the settings and artefacts will be arranged, so that this can be done quickly. If any changes need to be made during the programme, plan who will do this and when.

on the day before:

- check artefacts, materials, equipment, etc.
- if necessary, divide the children into groups and make group badges.

on the day:

- do not tell children what is going to take place.
- set up the hall.
- arrange artefacts.
- make any necessary last-minute preparations.
- ensure that group badges are worn.
- assume role and start programme.

MY LAND

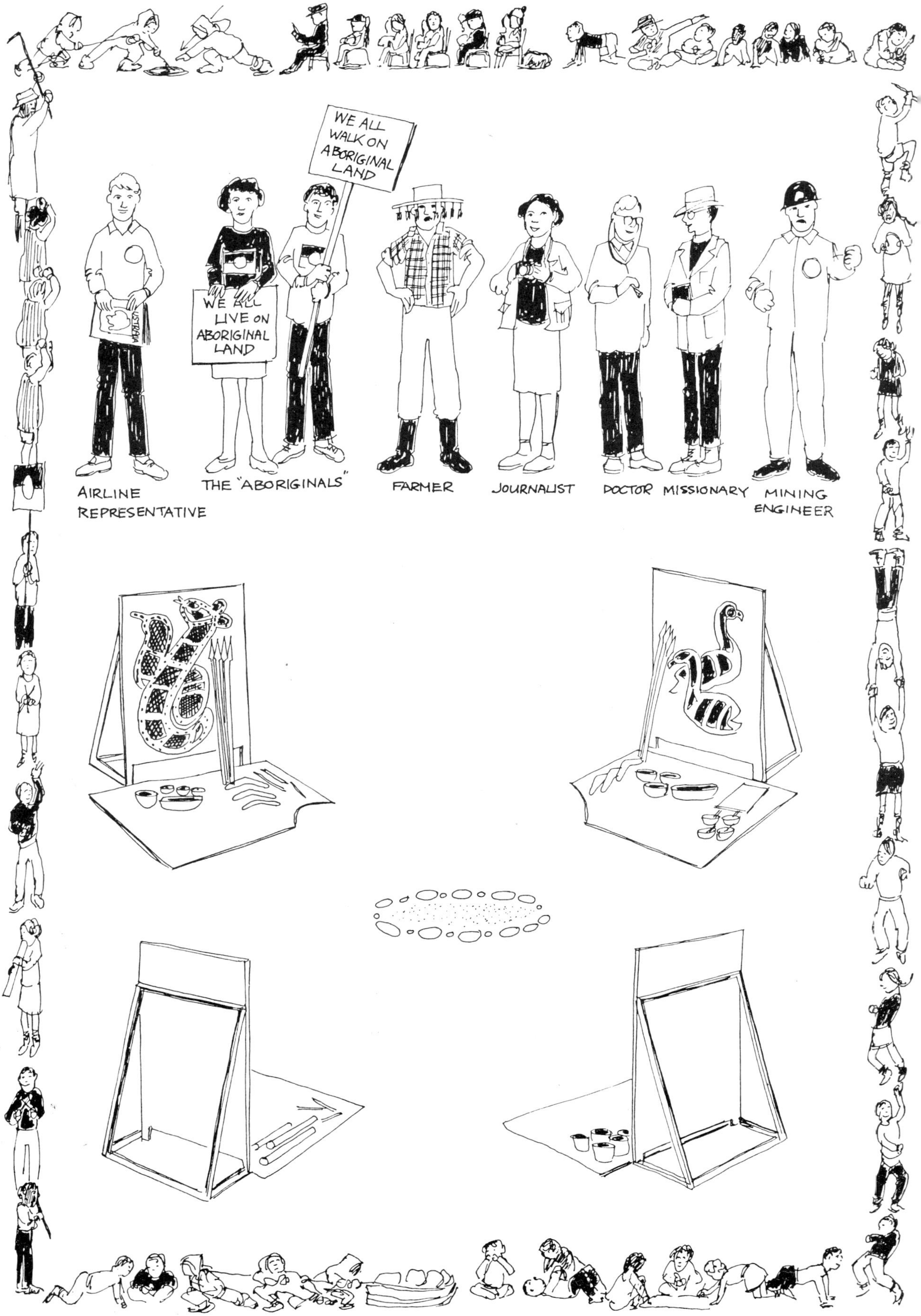
WE ALL
WALK ON
ABORIGINAL
LAND
WE ALL
LIVE ON
ABORIGINAL
LAND
AIRLINE
REPRESENTATIVE
THE "ABORIGINALS"
FARMER
JOURNALIST
DOCTOR
MISSIONARY
MINING
ENGINEER

Part Two. Programmes

MY LAND

Topic

The Topic for this programme is the Aboriginal people of Australia. It is one of a series of topics on *Different Ways of Living*, suggested by the World Wide Fund for Nature. The Australian Aborigines were chosen because their culture, with its values of harmony with the land, non-materialism, and community care, is far removed from that of the white people who control their country and also from the experience of the children participating.

Aim

The aim is to introduce children to a different and unfamiliar culture in order to widen their perception of the world. Through finding out how different a culture can be, they may be able to learn something about the multi-cultural society in which they are living.

Objectives

These are:

- to find out about a totally different cultural group by looking at lifestyle, customs, and beliefs.
- to learn about and try out different cultural activities, such as arts, crafts, storytelling, music.
- to examine a different climate, looking at the environment which it produces and the animals and vegetation which exist there.
- to compare the traditional way of living in harmony with the land with modern methods of mining, with the destruction of vegetation, and with overgrazing by non-indigenous animals.
- to look at the problems that arise when a traditional way of life is confronted by change and progress.
- to look at the problems of belonging to a minority group, particularly where that minority group is native to the country, unlike the majority.

Research

Useful addresses:

Survival International
310 Edgeware Road
London W2 1DY
Tel.: 01 723 5535
(Information about Aboriginal matters)

The Australian High Commission
Australia House
Strand
London WC2B 4LA
Tel.: 01 379 4334 (Information about Australia)

The Commonwealth Institute
Kensington High Street
London W8 6NQ
Tel.: 01 603 4535
(Information about Australia)

Museum of Mankind
Burlington Gardens
London W1X 2EX
Tel.: 01 437 2224
(Information about traditional Aboriginal life)

World Wide Fund for Nature
Panda House
Weyside Park
Godalming
Surrey GU7 1XR
Tel.: 04834 26444
(Information about flora and fauna)

Books and booklets

Australian National Commission for UNESCO (1974) *Australian Aboriginal Culture*, Canberra: Australian Government Publishing Service.
(Obtainable from Australian High Commission)

Baglin, Douglas and Mullins, Barbara (1984) *Aboriginals of Australia*, Sydney, Australia: Mulavon.
(Obtainable from the gift shop, Australia House)

Hughes, Jill (1979) *A Closer Look at Aborigines*, London: Hamish Hamilton.

Roberts, Janine (1978) *From Massacres to Mining*. The Colonization of Aboriginal Australia, London: CIMRA (Colonialism and Indigenous Minorities Research and Action) and War on Want.

Suter, Keith and Stearman, Kaye (1982) *Aboriginal Australians (Report No. 35)*, London: Minority Rights Group.

Audio/Visual
Aborigines and *Opening up Australia*
BBC Programmes for Schools
BBC Enterprises
Woodlands
80 Wood Lane
London W12 0TT
Tel: 01 743 5588
(Slides and cassette)
Tape of didjeridu music from Eric Maddern, Muriawgwifnion, Fachwen, Llanberis, Gwynedd LL55 3HB

Outline scenario

The basic outline of *My Land* is that the children will be taken, in imagination, on a journey to Australia, where they will meet and take part in the lives of the Aboriginal people who live there.

The settings will be four different areas of Australia.

Roles

There are ten roles in *My Land*. The original team consisted of five members but this is not essential. Adjustments can easily be made by changing names where necessary.

Remember that the team members should not attempt to make the children believe that they *are* Aboriginals but only that they are representing them, putting their point of view, and demonstrating how various aspects of Aboriginal life are carried out.

For a team of five:
(a) Airline representative.
Farmer.
Flying doctor.
Missionary.
Journalist.
Mining engineer.
(b) Amy.
(c) Kate.
(d) Julinga.
(e) David Jambajimba.

For a team of four:
(a) Airline representative.
David Jambajimba.
Farmer.

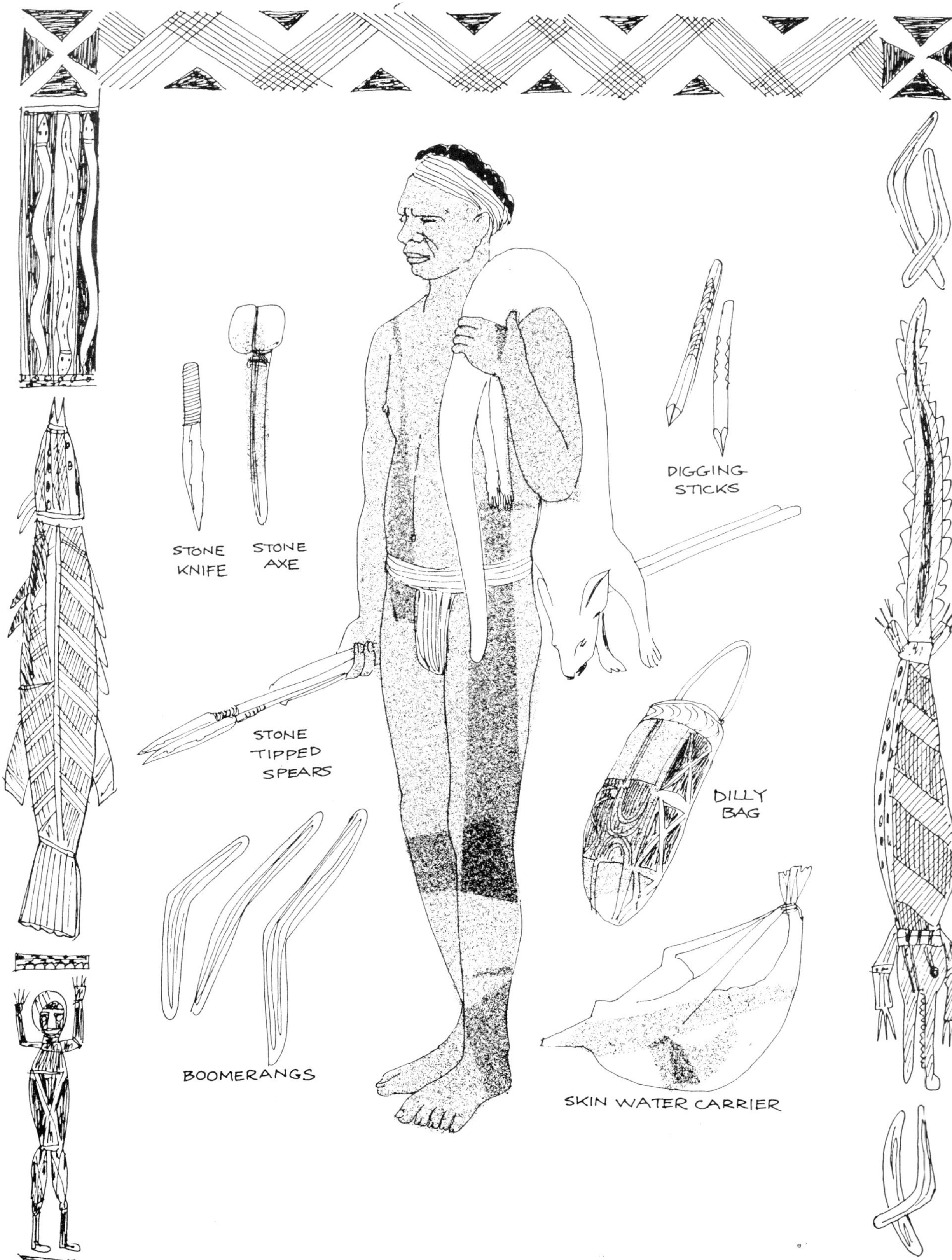
STONE KNIFE
STONE AXE
DIGGING STICKS
STONE TIPPED SPEARS
DILLY BAG
BOOMERANGS
SKIN WATER CARRIER

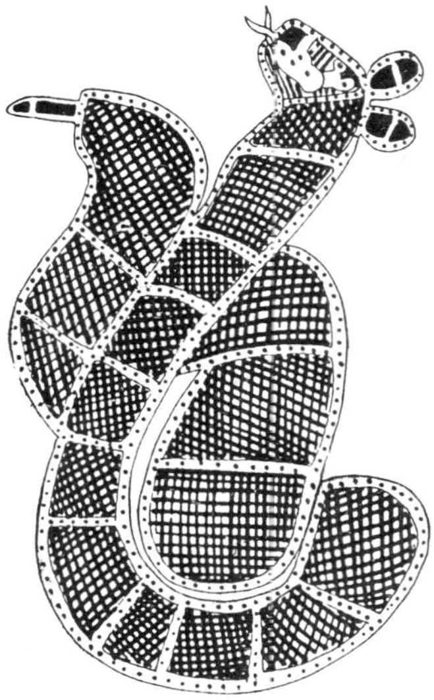

(b) Amy.
Flying doctor.
(c) Kate.
Missionary.
(d) Julinga.
Journalist.

One member of the team changes role during the corroboree to play the mining engineer.

For a team of three:
Leave out one of the groups, using as much material as possible from that group in the three remaining.

For a team of two:
Adapt the lesson plans (see p.62), sharing roles.

For one person only:
Use the lesson plans (see p.62) over a number of days or weeks.

The programme in detail

The programme can be divided into five parts:

Part A The beginning
Part B Aboriginal life (small-group work)
Part C Walkabout (large-group work)
Part D Corroboree (large-group work)
Part E The ending

Part A: The beginning
Location: Classroom
Role of team member: Airline representative.
Scenario: Team member A comes into the classroom and is introduced to the children as a representative of a well-known Australian airline, who will talk to them about Australia. The representative then shows slides, while asking questions and encouraging the children to share any information that they have about Australia.

Suggested slide sequence:
1 Map of Australia

Discussion
- smallest continent, largest island.
- how much larger than Great Britain?

2 Captain Cook

Discussion
- When did he 'discover' Australia?

3 Australian animals (kangaroo, koala bear, duck-billed platypus, frilled neck lizard, etc.)

Discussion
- Difference from animals in other parts of the world.
- Introduction of term 'marsupial'.

4 The Land (Ayers Rock, the Barrier Reef, open cast mining)

Discussion
- Tourist attractions.
- Mineral wealth.

5 Sport and Leisure (surfing, barbeques, etc.)

Discussion
- Compare with leisure activities in this country.

6 The Australian flag

Discussion
- Reason for its design.

OPEN CAST MINING

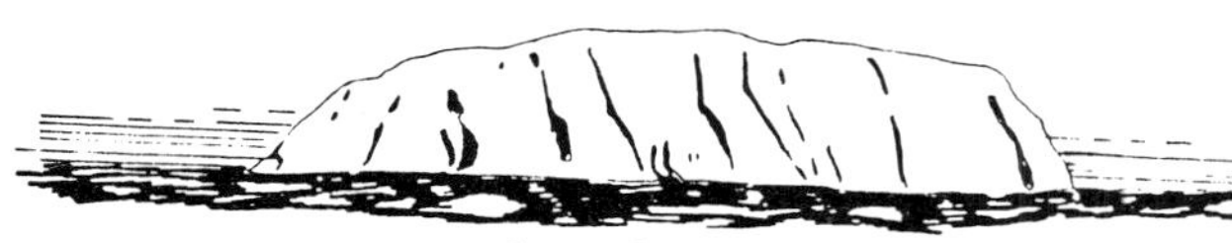

AYERS ROCK

During the discussion of the last slide, Amy suddenly steps out from her hiding place and addresses the children.

Information
- She is an Aboriginal from Australia on holiday in this country.
- She has been listening to the airline representative and feels angry that he has not once referred to the Aboriginal people of Australia.
- When talking about Captain Cook, he forgot to mention that, when Cook arrived in the country, there were already people living there, the Aboriginals, who had been there for forty thousand years.
- Amy writes the word AB-ORIGINAL on the board.

Discussion
- What do the children think it means?

Information
- When the settlers arrived, they did not ask to share the land with the Aboriginals but killed many of them.

- The importance of the land to her people; how they live in harmony with it, never taking more from it than is necessary for survival.
- The significance of Uluru (the Aboriginal name for Ayers Rock). Uluru is a very sacred site for her people. In the caves at the bottom of the rock, the walls are covered in paintings and carvings which date back for more than ten thousand years.
- The importance of the Dreamtime stories, which have been handed down from generation to generation, and which tell the people how they should live in harmony with the land and where they can find food and fresh water.

Amy invites the children to visit Australia with her to meet her people. They accept and are each given a colour-coded ticket by the airline representative, who will go with them.
The journey is represented by walking along the school corridor, which is decorated with travel posters and airline signs, to the hall where the children then meet the rest of the team.

Part B: Aboriginal life
Location: Hall.
Setting: In the centre of the hall is a circle of stones enclosing an area of fine sand. In each corner of the hall, a mat is laid in front of a painted screen showing the totem animal of that group. The artefacts for each group are laid out on the mat.

Roles of Team Members — Aboriginals
Scenario: The children enter the hall.
Kate, Julinga, and David sit in the middle of the central area, which is their sacred site. They hold land-rights banners and are chanting 'We all live on Aboriginal land'.
Amy introduces the children, saying that they have come from Great Britain.
Julinga welcomes them and explains the flag which they carry: 'Black for the colour of our skins, red for the land and for the blood which has been shed, yellow is the great sun which unites the people to the land.'
Kate asks if the children are here to join the land-rights demonstration.
Amy replies that they have come to learn about traditional Aboriginal culture and what life is like for Aboriginals today.
The children are allocated to groups according to the colour of their tickets.

General group work
Much of the small-group work is similar because all of the children need to learn the basic facts about Aboriginal life. These are presented in an individual way by each team member.
General group work includes:

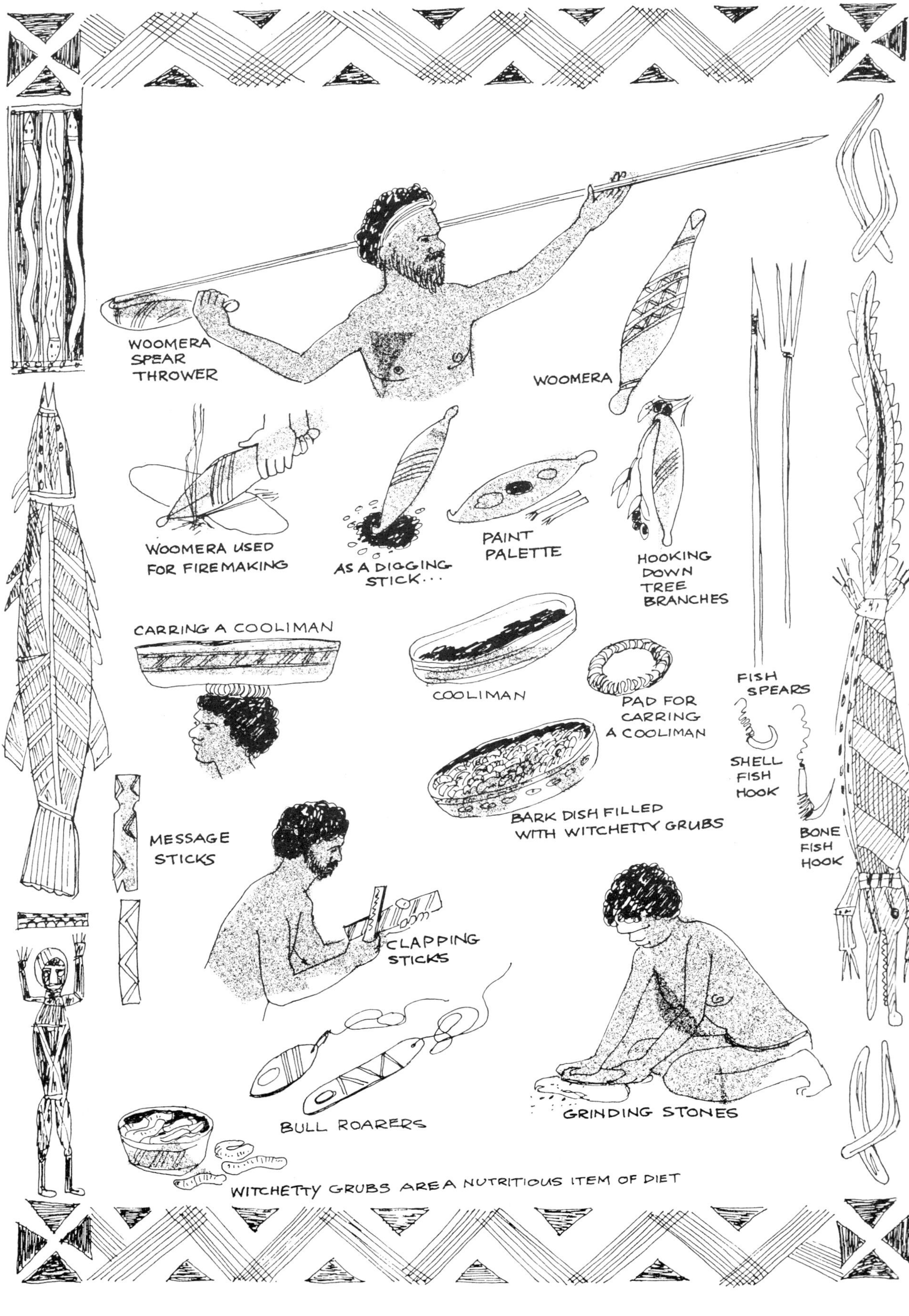
WOOMERA
SPEAR
THROWER
WOOMERA
WOOMERA USED
FOR FIREMAKING
AS A DIGGING
STICK...
PAINT
PALETTE
HOOKING
DOWN
TREE
BRANCHES
CARRING A COOLIMAN
COOLIMAN
PAD FOR
CARRING
A COOLIMAN
FISH
SPEARS
SHELL
FISH
HOOK
BONE
FISH
HOOK
BARK DISH FILLED
WITH WITCHETTY GRUBS
MESSAGE
STICKS
CLAPPING
STICKS
BULL ROARERS
GRINDING STONES
WITCHETTY GRUBS ARE A NUTRITIOUS ITEM OF DIET

1 Background

Stimulus
- Picture album.

Discussion
- The different types of Aboriginals, indicating that they came from different parts of the country.

Information
- Where the people of that group came from, shown on a map of Australia in the album.

Stimulus
- Photographs of landscape, showing what kind of land the Aboriginal people lived in (very hot and dry).

Discussion
- How the land influenced their way of life.

2 The land

Stimulus
- The artefacts that comprised the possessions of an Aboriginal family.

Discussion
- Comparison with the number of possessions that we need.

Information
- How nomadic life is one long search for water and food in season; moving on so that not too much is taken from any area.

Discussion
- Comparison with our lifestyle, farming, etc.

3 Traditions

Stimulus
- Telling of group's Dreamtime story. See illustration group work.

Activities
- Painting a picture of the Dreamtime creature while listening to the story.

Information
- The Dreamtime tradition. Each group had its own story and also songs which told about the wanderings of its totem animal in mythological times. These songs were handed down from generation to generation.

Discussion
- Do we have similar stories?

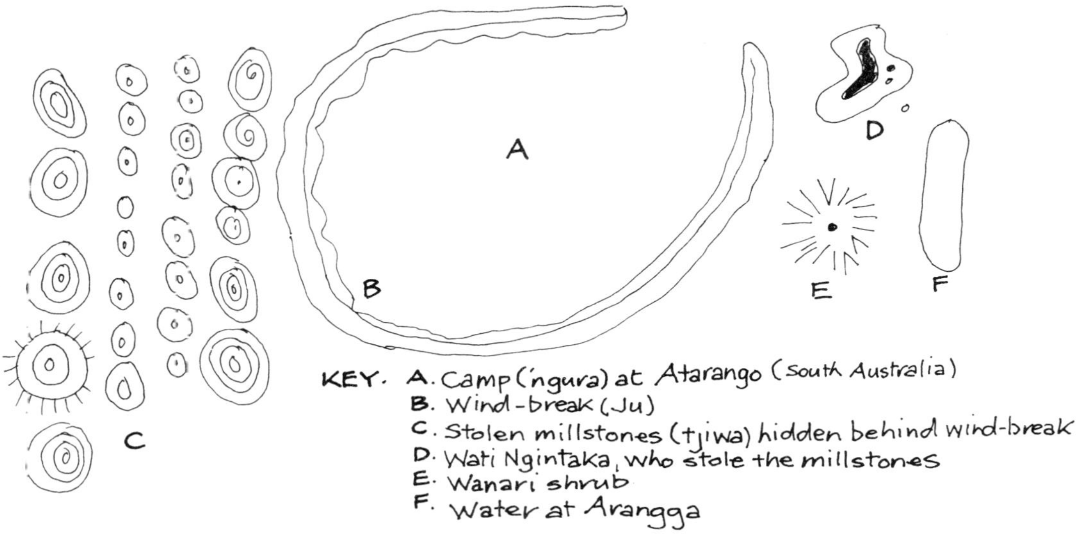

This is a drawing of a song map. It tells the story of NGINTAKA — the Lizard Ancestor who went secretly into the lands of the East to steal some millstones. Leaving his home he travelled unseen through the lands of other people. He stole the millstones from a place called Walada. As he sneaked his way homewards he camped for the night at Atarango. When he moved off he passed a big pool of water. Can you see his camp, the stolen millstones behind the wind-break and the pool he passed? The song goes on to tell of his adventures in another territory where, in the hills near the mountains, he found a large cave. His wife dug holes near to the opening of the cave. When it was dark, men, kangaroos and dogs came to drink from the water that had gathered in the holes. Helped by his nephew PARARUKO, he killed them all. Pararuko later changed into a desert oak and remained there by the cave.

This type of map not only told a Dreamtime story to entertain people, but it also described the Dreaming tracks along which they would travel. It gave practical information about the countryside — where water and shelter could be found and what sort of animals and plants could be seen.

Information

- Activities of childhood. Fetching water, making boomerangs, practising spear throwing with toy spear, drawing in the sand, playing chasing games, chewing kangaroo bones to make mince for the sick or very old to eat.

Discussion and information

- Comparison with their own childhood activities.
- Adulthood; the importance of preparation for becoming an adult.
- Learning of sacred stories and the law.
- Boys had to show that they were brave, self-disciplined, and respectful.
- Girls taught about motherhood.

- A girl was not considered a woman until she had had two children.
- No chief in a group but older men became elders who had special responsibility for the keeping of the laws.
- Old age and death; old people were highly respected.
- When someone died there was much wailing and crying; women covered themselves with white powder, men cut their thighs with sharp stones.
- Burial customs different in different parts of the country; some buried the body in earth, some put the body on a platform or in a tree, some cremated their dead.

4 Food

Stimulus
- Spears, woomeras, boomerangs, digging sticks.

Activities
- Learning how to use hunting weapons and digging sticks.
- Learning about tracking and stalking.

Information
- Different ways of getting food.
- How we get our food.
- Importance of never taking more than necessary.

Discussion
- Difference between hunting for food and hunting for pleasure or profit.

5 Music and dance

Stimulus
- Tape of Aboriginal music.

Information
- The didjeridu is used in Northern Australia.

Activities
- Using clapping sticks or boomerangs to beat out rhythms.
- Learning the land-rights chant. "We all live on Aboriginal land".
- Devising a dance or 'stamp' which represents the group's totem animal.

6 Art

Stimulus
- Screen

Information
- Pigments used in painting (earth colours: red, yellow, white, black) and where they come from.
- Use of chewed twigs for painting.
- What is painted? (rocks, bark, boomerangs, didjeridus, etc.).

Activity
- Finish paintings which were started during telling of Dreamtime story.

7 Coming of white settlers

Stimulus

- Picture of chained Aboriginals

Information

- Cruelty of people in eighteenth century, transportation, etc.

Discussion

- Lack of understanding and fear of the unknown, then and now.

Information

- Attempts to exterminate Aboriginals by sending out hunting parties. None left in Tasmania.
- Introduction of diseases previously unknown.
- Effect of introduction of alcohol to people who had never experienced it before.
- Taking of children into mission schools in order to 'save' them, causing them to grow up belonging to neither world.

Discussion

- The problems of people who are faced with changes in the world around them.

Information

- The Aboriginals believe that the land should be used by whoever lives on it. Much of it is sacred to them.
- The Australian Government wishes to extract minerals from the land.

Discussion
Whose land is it?

Special group work
Group 1 The Barkundji people from New South Wales
Group leader: Julinga.
Dreamtime Story: The Black Swans.

A long time ago there lived two white swans. They were a beautiful sight as they glided across the still water of the lake. Just to watch them would have filled you with a sense of peace and happiness.

One day the peace and stillness was disturbed by some Eagle Hawks. They swooped down and attacked the swans, pecking at their eyes and pulling out their feathers.

Circling high above, in the clear air, watching what was happening, were two Mountain Crows. They had no love for the Eagle Hawks and soon chased them away. The Mountain Crows took pity on the swans and covered them with some of their own black feathers to keep them warm during the cold nights.

Cared for by the crows, the swans recovered slowly and, at last, recovered their beauty. But now their feathers had all become gleaming black like those that the crows had lent them. The blood which had flowed from their eyes when they were pecked by the Eagle Hawks had run down and stained their beaks a bright red and the blood from their torn legs had stained their feet. That is why, to this day, the swans in New South Wales are black with blood-red beaks and feet.

Special emphasis: The relationship with the land.

Information
- The land was like a mother to the Aboriginals and they were careful not to harm it.
- If they obeyed the laws they would always be blessed with children, food and water.
- They burned small areas in a controlled way to encourage new growth.
- They spat out seeds to ensure next year's growth of plants.
- They kept the water holes clean and clear.
- They always left enough of a plant to ensure next year's growth.
- In some parts, no plant was taken after flowering; it was then a 'motherplant' and was left, undisturbed, to scatter its seeds.

Activities
- Making of bark paintings.
- Making of fern decorations for the 'corroboree' later in the programme (using real ferns or cut-out green paper ferns).

Encounter with farmer (team member a)

Discussion

- Farmer accuses the Aboriginals of starting bush fires. The children are able to explain about the reason for the fires and how they are always under control.
- Children explain the Aboriginal attitude to the land.
- Julinga questions the wisdom of the introduction of sheep which overgraze the land.

Group 2 The Kabi people from Queensland
Group leader: Amy
Dreamtime story: The Tortoise and the Echidna.

In the beginning there were two women who travelled from the north in search of a home. They were Echidna woman and her baby and the long-necked Tortoise woman. Echidna carried with her a large, flat stone and the Tortoise woman carried a bunch of spears.

One day they arrived at a pleasant place where they decided to make camp. Echidna went out hunting, leaving her baby in the care of Tortoise. Echidna was away for a long time and Tortoise became more and more hungry. Eventually, she could bear it no longer and ate Echidna's baby. She then felt so full that she fell fast asleep.

When Echidna returned, she searched everywhere for her baby. She shook Tortoise awake and asked her where the baby was. Tortoise said that she supposed that the baby must have been eaten by a dog but Echidna noticed that Tortoise looked very full. She asked, 'Tortoise, did you eat my baby?' Tortoise had to admit that she had. She tried to run away but Echidna caught her and beat her with a stick till she fell on the ground. Echidna then threw her flat stone which landed on Tortoise's back. Tortoise then threw her bundle of spears at Echidna and hit her in the back.

From that moment, Tortoise has always carried a heavy shell on her back, and Echidna, who is a type of porcupine, is covered in quills. They no longer travel together. Tortoise now lives beside the billabong and Echidna found her home in dry rocky land.

Special emphasis: Beliefs, Drama and Dance, Animals.

Information

- Animals of Australia, before and after the settlers.
- Uluru (Ayers Rock), the caves and paintings found there and its importance as a sacred site.
- Customs and beliefs.

Activities

- Acting out Dreamtime story.
- Devising dances from the movements and habits of the kangaroo.
- Uses of cooliman; carrying one on the head.
- Making and use of a dillybag (see instructions).

GIRL FETCHING WATER
SPEAR THROWING WITH TOY SPEARS
OLD PEOPLE WERE HIGHLY RESPECTED
WHEN SOMEONE DIED THERE WAS MUCH WAILING AND CRYING

Encounter with Missionary (team member a)
Invites Amy to church meeting.
She tells of how she was taken from her parents as a small child and brought up at a mission school; of how she now feels that she belongs to neither world, but wishes to keep to the old beliefs.
The children should be able to tell the missionary about some of these.

Group 3 The Pini people from Western Australia
Group leader: Kate.
Dreamtime story: The Crow and the Eagle Hawk.

A long time ago the Crow lived with its uncle, the great Eagle Hawk, and each took its turn at hunting. One day the Eagle Hawk sent the Crow to hunt for wallaby. The greedy crow caught a fine fat wallaby but ate all of the meat itself. On returning it told the Eagle Hawk that it had had no luck. 'You are looking remarkably well fed' said the Eagle Hawk. 'That is because I was so hungry that I ate some acacia gum' replied the Crow. The Eagle Hawk did not believe this and started to tickle the Crow. At first the Crow laughed but then it was very sick, and the Eagle Hawk saw that it was indeed full of wallaby meat. The Eagle Hawk was so angry that it rolled the Crow in the hot ashes of the fire, turning its feathers black and making its eyes red, and that is how it has remained to this day. Since then the crow has never been allowed to hunt for itself, but can only live off carrion — a dead animal — which is killed by some other creature.

Special emphasis: Home-based activities, Medicine and magic.

Information
- Gathering of food; what was found on, above, and under the ground.

Activities
- Use of digging stick.
- Search for 'witchetty grubs'.

Information
- Preparation of food.

Activity
- Grinding corn between stones.

Information
- How fire came to man (see story, *The Crocodile and the Rainbow Bird*).

Information
- Carrying of firesticks.

Activity
- Trying to make fire with hardwood stick and flat stone, on which are dried leaves.

THE CROCODILE AND THE RAINBOW BIRD

Once upon a time, a long time ago the crocodile was the only creature to have fire. He lay there in his scaly skin close by his fire and growled at every creature "I will not give you my fire, you will have to eat your food raw"
The rainbow bird looked down at the crocodile and thought "Keer-ook if I fly down I can take fire and give it to man". So he waited until the crocodile yawned and his eyes were closed and at long last he was asleep. The rainbow bird flew down and snatched the firestick. The crocodile woke up and roared out "Bring back my fire", but the rainbow bird flew away and into the heart of every tree he put fire. The crocodile from then onwards was doomed always to be cold and wet and the little bit of fire that was left over went into the rainbow bird's tail

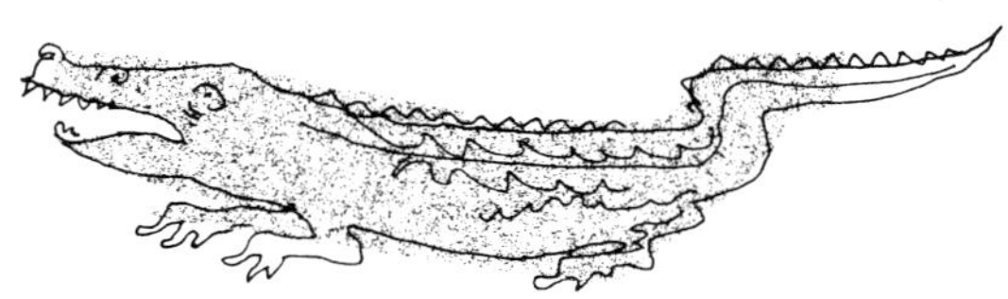

SWINGING A BULL ROARER

MESSAGE STICK

Information

- Medicine and magic.
  Traditional healer very respected, used natural things around him to cure illness — ashes rubbed into wounds to help them to heal, colds treated with boiled tea-tree leaves, etc.
- Tying a band of material round the head to cure headache.
- Coming of settlers brought new diseases for which there were no Aboriginal cures.
- Healer also used magic to cure illness. He used good magic, such as the bringing of rain, and bad magic, such as putting a curse on someone who had broken the laws. This was done by pointing a bone at the guilty person and later chanting special songs. To remove bad magic, a stronger healer had to be found.

Encounter with Flying Doctor (team member a)
Doctor wants to know if anyone is ill.
Kate replies that they have their own plant or other 'bush remedies' for many sicknesses. The children should be able to tell the Doctor about some of these.
Before the settlers arrived, the Aboriginals had very little illness.
Comparison between the doctor's remedy for headache (aspirin) and Kate's (tying a band around the forehead).

Group 4 The Tiwi people from Northern Australia
Group leader: David Jambajimba.
Dreamtime story: The Rainbow Serpent.

In the beginning, when all the land was flat and bare, the Rainbow Serpent awoke from her slumbers, deep within the earth. as she pushed her way upwards, she created the hills and mountains. As she made her way slowly across the land, the winding tracks she left became the rivers and the valleys. Wherever she went, she provided water and the plants and animals which make up our food.

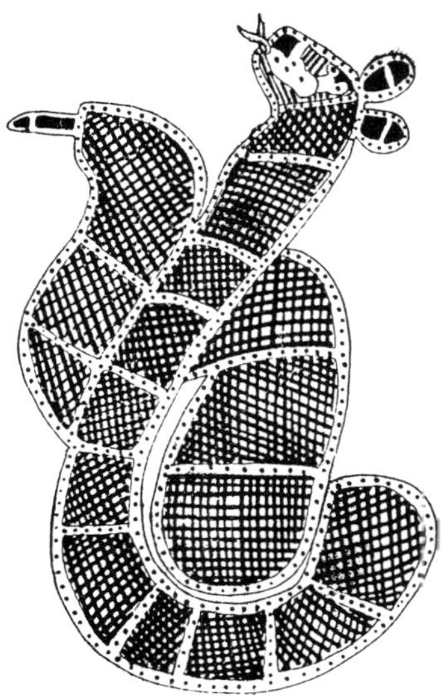

Special emphasis: Hunting and fishing, music.

Information

- Importance of taking only what is necessary when hunting.
- Sharing of proceeds of hunt with those unable to hunt for themselves.
- Never killing a totem animal.

Activities

- Hunting expedition, tracking, stalking, camouflage, walking silently.
- Use of woomera (spear thrower).
- Uses of boomerang.
- Fishing expedition, using different methods — line and hook, stunning with stone dropped from a height, using crayfish held in hand as bait.

CARPET PYTHON
KOALA
GREAT GREY KANGAROO
DUCK-BILLED PLATYPUS
FRILL NECK LIZARD
STENCIL PAINTINGS
CAVE PAINTINGS
LEGENDARY HERO INGALADDI
WANDJINA PAINTING

Demonstration
- Playing of didjeridu, or mime of playing to taped music.

Activities
- Making didjeridus out of cardboard tubes.
- Painting designs on didjeridu.

Information
- Special celebrations.
- Use of bullroarer for summoning the people to a gathering.

Encounter with Journalist (team member a)
Journalist wants to know what the children have been learning.
Takes posed photographs of children hunting.
David asks him to go away, as they would prefer journalists and tourists not to intrude on the lives of the Aboriginals.

Information
- Use of message sticks.

Activity
- A member of the group takes the message stick to the next group; waits on edge of group until invited to give the message.

Scenario: The message stick is explained by the team leader. It is a pictorial invitation to a festival or corroboree. A child from that group is then sent to give the message stick to the next group, who in turn send someone to take it to another group, and so on.

When the group work is finished:
- the stamps are practised.
- clapping sticks and boomerangs are shared out.
- faces are decorated with face paint.
- Barkundji people decorate their arms and legs with ferns.

Part C: Walkabout
Location: As for small-group work.
Scenario: Corners are tidied, artefacts are arranged on floor beside screen, mats are rolled up, and the children set out on a walkabout (journey) to meet the other groups, to see their artefacts, and to hear about each other's Dreamings. The mats are relaid to fit around the central circle of sand, in such a way that they create the Aboriginal flag.

Part D: Corroboree
Extra role: Mining engineer (team member a).
Scenario: The children sit around the outer edge of their mats. The team leader of the Tiwi group welcomes the other groups and explains more about the corroboree.

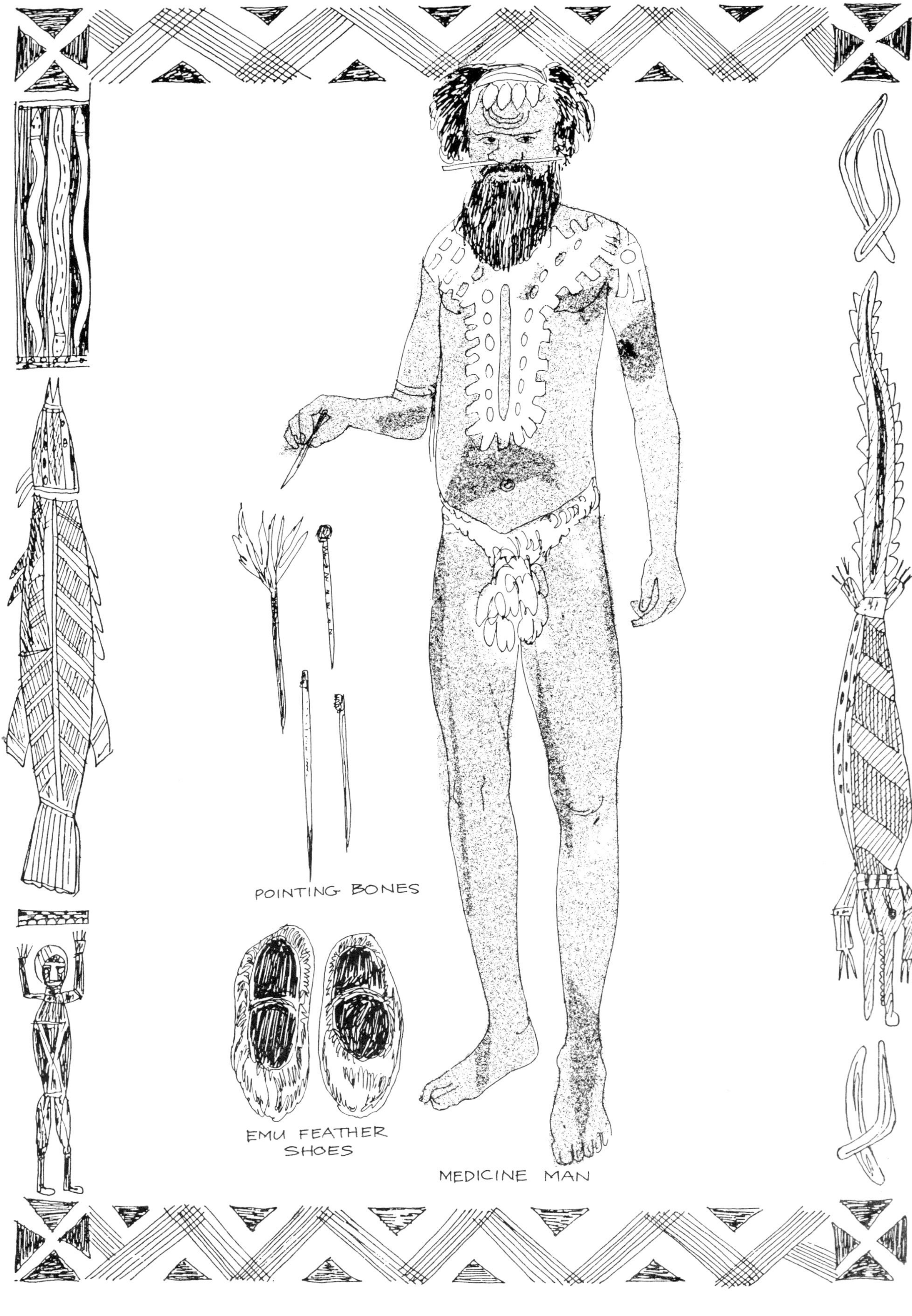
POINTING BONES
EMU FEATHER SHOES
MEDICINE MAN

Activities

- The Tiwi group introduce themselves — 'We are the Tiwi people and we come from the Northern Territory.' Each group then does the same in turn.
- Paintings are shown.
- Each group performs its stamp in turn, accompanied by clapping sticks and didjeridu.
- All groups join in together, dancing from the edge of their mats towards the centre of the sand circle.

Scenario: There is a sudden interruption. A mining engineer storms in, demanding that the land should be cleared. This leads to a confrontation between the Aboriginals and the engineer. The children move to one side during the discussion.

The engineer says that he has permission from the Government to mine the land. He says that the land belongs to the Government, not to them.

The Aboriginals say that the land is sacred and that they belong to it, not it to them.

The engineer leaves, giving them thirty minutes to clear the site.

The Aboriginals sit down on the sacred site, holding their banners.

One team member 'de-roles' and takes the children back to their classroom.

Part E: The ending

Discussion

- Team member asks children about their feelings and reactions.

Scenario: The children are asked if they would like to question the mining engineer.
The engineer puts his case (metals needed for making cars, vital equipment for hospitals, etc.)
The children question ('hot seat') the engineer.
Engineer answers the questions and leaves.
The children are asked to 'de-role', and to think about and discuss what they have experienced, the attitudes of the Aboriginals and of the engineer, and their own feelings, etc.

Follow-up work

The programme should be followed up in depth by the teacher, using the *My Land* Resource Pack and other sources of information. Follow-up work may be directed towards any subject across the curriculum. This particular programme is a good way in to multi-cultural studies.
The topic could be extended by the children arranging a corroboree for another class or else presenting the whole programme to another class, by taking on the roles and using the artefacts that were made for the original programme.

MAKING A DILLY BAG

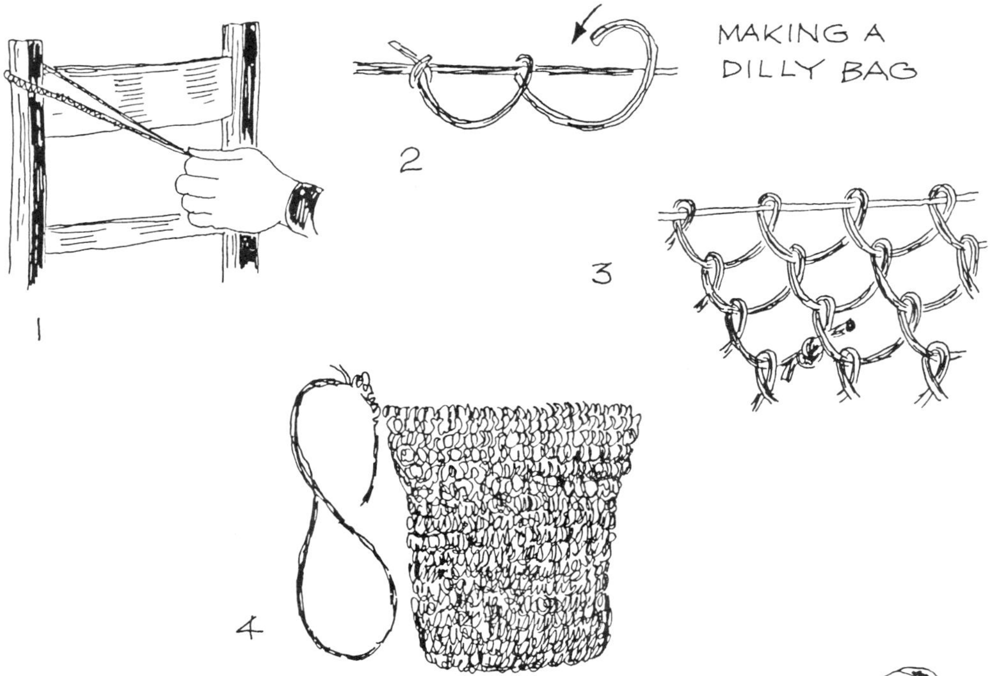

A DIDJERIDU CAN BE MADE OUT OF A CARDBOARD TUBE. THE BLOWING END COULD BE REINFORCED WITH PLASTER OF PARIS

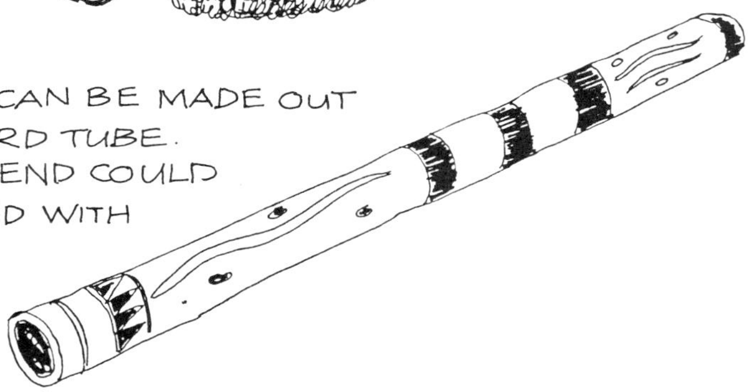

COOLIMAN CAN BE MADE OUT OF PAPER MACHE

BOOMERANG CAN BE MADE OUT OF CARD BEND UP SLIGHTLY AT ONE END

Practical organisation

Costume

Airline representative: dark skirt or trousers, white shirt, and an 'airline' badge.
'Aboriginals': skirts or casual trousers, tee-shirts with Aboriginal flag or land-rights emblem.
Farmer: hat and boots.
Journalist: casual jacket, camera.
Flying doctor: white coat, stethoscope.
Missionary: linen jacket, dog-collar, straw hat.
Mining engineer: overalls, hard hat.

Settings

Make a plan of the hall lay-out. A colleague or friend may be willing to paint the Dreamtime creatures on screens or large sheets of paper for the four groups. If not, the children can paint them during the preliminary practical work.

Artefacts, materials, and equipment

The artefacts listed below are those that were used in the original programme but teachers should use whatever they find available or feel is necessary. Some artefacts may be improvised, omitted, or replaced by illustrations.

Part A

- projector.
- slides of Australian tourist attractions (see p.39); if it not possible to obtain slides, use a series of pictures of Australian scenes.
- screen.
- board and chalk.
- colour-coded tickets.
- travel posters.
- airline signs.

Part B

- stones.
- sand.
- banners with land-rights slogans.
- aboriginal flag.
- message stick.

For all groups:

- mat or carpet cut to fit around central area.
- album containing pictures of Aboriginal people (obtained from books or the Commonwealth Institute or the gift shop at Australia House), maps, landscape, etc.
- face paint.
- sugar paper.
- clapping sticks.
- paint (red, yellow, white, black) in papier mâché bowls (made by children).

- painting sticks.
- hunting spears (made out of bamboo).
- woomeras.
- coolimans (made by children).
- digging sticks.
- boomerangs (see instructions).

For Group 1:
- screen with painting of Black Swan.
- ferns, or green paper and scissors.
- bark for painting.

For Group 2:
- screen with painting of Tortoise.
- pad of material for carrying cooliman.
- string for making dilly bags (see instructions).

For Group 3:
- screen with painting of Crow.
- grinding stones.
- 'witchetty grubs' (boiled pasta shells).
- hardwood stick for fire making.
- strip of leather for headache cure.

For Group 4:
- screen with painting of Rainbow Serpent.
- fish spears.
- fish hooks.
- tape of didjeridu music (for address, see p.37).
- cardboard tubes (for making didjeridus).
- bullroarer.

Make a detailed list of how you will obtain the various items: what can be found in school, what can be borrowed, what you and your colleagues will make, what the children can make, etc.

Preliminary practical session
This should be carried out without revealing to the children what will happen during the programme.
Materials

- large pieces of paper or material (for the mats).
- if making screens, large pieces of paper or card.
- paint.
- pieces of wood dowel (for clapping sticks).
- newspaper, paste (for papier mâché coolimans and bowls).
- card, scissors, etc.
- strings for dillybags.

The children are divided into four groups: Pini, Kabi, Barkundji, and Tiwi.

Each group should make:

- a coloured mat (In total, there should be two black, two red).
- screen or large painting of Dreamtime creature for settings.
- one or two coolimans.
- four bowls.
- a dillybag.
- two or three sets of clapping sticks.
- two or three boomerangs.

Each child should make:

- a group badge with a picture of group Dreamtime creature.

On the day before
Check artefacts, scenery, and costumes.
Boil pasta shells to make 'witchetty grubs'.

On the day
Do not tell the children what is going to take place. This is most important.
Set out hall.
Hide 'witchetty grubs', wrapped in packing straw, under mat in Pini corner.
Take children out of classroom, set up projector, and conceal 'Amy'.
Bring children back to classroom where they put on group badges.
Introduce the airline representative.
While the first part of the programme is taking place, a member of the team should display the travel posters along the corridor between the classroom and the hall.

BARK PAINTINGS

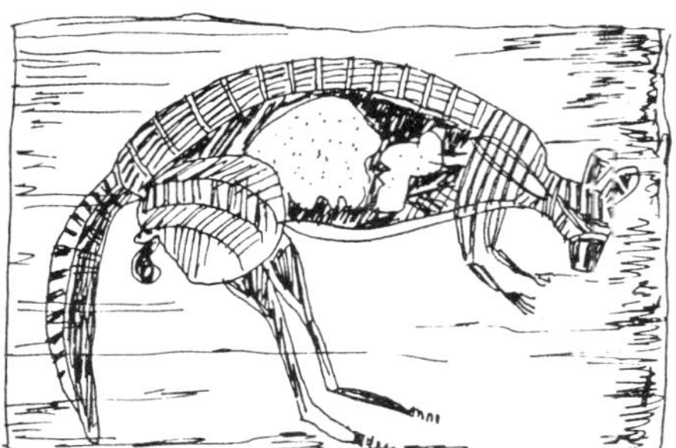

KANGAROO

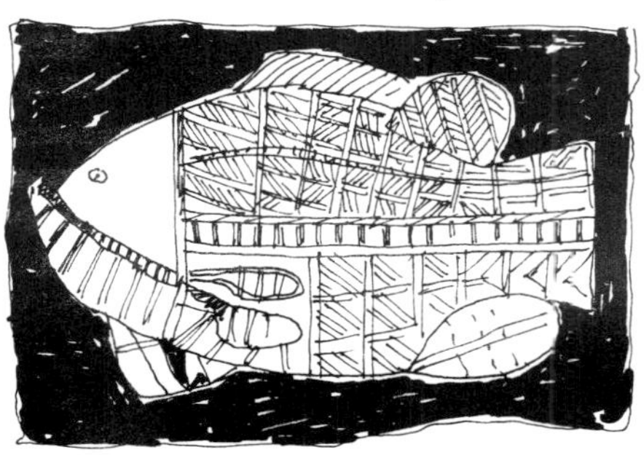

BARRAMUNDI FISH

MASASSAN PRAU FEATURED ON ARNHEM LAND BARK

Lesson Plans

These are for the teacher who wishes to tackle this topic single-handed or with one colleague. The teacher may take all roles or they may be shared. Roles may be assumed by changing one or two items of costume, perhaps behind a screen. Costume need not be elaborate but may be suggested by one or two items. Some ideas are given.

Some authentic artefacts may be available from contacts but it is possible to use a combination of illustrations and improvisation. Most of the equipment which is suggested is available in schools.

These plans make constant reference to various parts of the programme, *My Land*, described above.

Lesson 1
Location: classroom.
Role of teacher: (a) airline representative.
(b) Present day Aboriginal.
Costume: (a) airline badge.
(b) tee-shirt with Aboriginal flag or land-rights slogan.

Materials and equipment:
- Screen
- Projector
- Set of slides of tourist Australia.
- If projector unavailable, pictures of tourist Australia.
- Board and chalk.
- Paper and pencil for each child.

The teacher starts in the role of airline representative and the lesson follows, exactly, Part 1 of the programme described above, until the showing of the Australian flag. The children are asked to draw the flag. While they are doing this, the teacher leaves the room and re-appears a few minutes later, wearing a land-rights tee-shirt, in the role of an Aboriginal. The remainder of the lesson is as in the original programme. It ends with the children being invited to visit Australia to find out about Aboriginal life.

Lessons 2 and 3
Location: Classroom, arranged so that four groups can have their own space to work, preferably sitting on the floor.
Role of teacher: Present day Aboriginal, as in Lesson 1.
Costume: As in Lesson 1.

Materials:
- Cardboard.
- Cardboard rolls.
- Scissors.

- Paint (red, yellow, white, black).
- Sticks for painting.
- Large sheets of paper.
- Newspaper and paste for papier mâché.
- Pictures of Aboriginal rock paintings.
- Pictures of Aboriginals using didjeridus and boomerangs.

Theme: The Dreamtime, Art.

Stimulus: Rock paintings.

Information:
- Paint and where it was obtained (red and yellow ochre ground from rocks, white from white clay, black made from charcoal).
- Brushes were made by chewing ends of twigs.

Divide class into four groups: the Barkundji, Tiwi, Pini, and Kabi people. The same groups will be used in other lessons. The teacher, in role as a modern Aboriginal, moves from group to group.

Practical work:
- Making papier mâché bowls for paint and large carrying dishes (coolimans).
- While children are working, take each group in turn and read or tell the children that group's Dreamtime story. (See *Special groupwork*, pp.48-49.)
- When the papier mâché is completed, children can design and paint a picture of their Dreamtime creature.

Stimulus: Pictures of Aboriginals using didjeridus and boomerangs.

Practical work:
- Making and decorating of didjeridus, boomerangs, and a message stick.
- Each group should make a mat out of material or card. Two should be painted red, the other two black. These will be used in Lesson 8.

Lesson 4

Location: Hall or large classroom.
Role of teacher: (a) Aboriginal hunter.
(b) Farmer.
Costume: (a) Tracksuit, or as in Lesson 1.
(b) Hat and wellington boots.

Artefacts:
- Spears/Fish Spears (made from bamboo).
- Woomera or spear thrower (real if possible, or make a copy or use a picture).
- Boomerangs (real if available, or use those made in previous lesson).
- Digging sticks (about 60 cm in length).
- Boiled pasta shells ('witchetty grubs') wrapped in packing straw — these should be hidden in the hall before the lesson.

Theme: Food — hunting and gathering, care of the land.

Information:
- Type of food eaten by Aboriginals in the past (see Food, p.46).
- Use of digging sticks; search for witchetty grubs, as in Pini group work, p.61.
- Care of the land (see *THE LAND*, p.43 and Barkundji group work, p.48).

Activities: Hunting and fishing expeditions, as in Tiwi group work, p.53.

Information:
- Tracking and hunting methods.
- Different methods of fishing (see Tiwi group work, p.53).

Confrontation: Teacher in role as Farmer.
Discussion: As in the Barkundji group work, p.49.

Lesson 5
Location: Classroom.
Role of teacher: (a) Aboriginal who was brought up in a mission school.
(b) Missionary from fifty years ago.

Costume: (a) As in Lesson 1.
(b) Linen jacket, dog-collar, panama hat.

Artefacts:
- Paintings done in Lesson 3.
- Bullroarer.

Theme:
- Traditions and beliefs — childhood, adulthood, old age, death, etc., as in *Traditions*, p.43-46.
- Children show pictures of their Dreamtime creatures. Each Group tells the rest of the class its own Dreamtime story.

Information and discussion:
- Aboriginal leader tells children about her childhood at a mission school and how she now belongs to neither world.
- Traditions, as on p.43-46.

Confrontation:
- Teacher in role as Missionary.
- Missionary tries to take children into mission school.
- Children tell missionary that Aboriginal people have their own beliefs which they do not want to lose. They describe some of these.

Lesson 6
Location: Classroom.
Role of teacher: (a) Aboriginal.
(b) Flying Doctor.

Costume: (a) As in Lesson 1.
(b) White coat, stethoscope.

Artefacts and materials:

- Grinding stones.
- Ears of grains.
- Coolimans (made in Lesson 2/3).
- Hardwood stick, dried leaves, and stone for fire-making.
- Strip of material for headache cure.

Theme: Home-based activities, medicine, and magic.
Information and activities:
- Fire-making and grinding of grain, as in Pini group work, p.51.
- Different uses of cooliman.

Information: Aboriginal cures and remedies, as in Pini group, work, p.53.

Discussion: Comparisons with the children's experience of medicine and any knowledge of folk medicine.

Confrontation: Teacher in role as Flying Doctor.

Discussion: Comparison between Aboriginal and Western medicine, as in Pini group work, p.53.

Lesson 7
Location: Hall.

Role of teacher: Aboriginal.

Costume: As in Lesson 1.

Artefacts:
- Didjeridus (made in Lesson 2).
- Several pairs of clapping sticks (20 cm lengths of hardwood such as 12.5 mm dowel).

Theme: Music and dance.
Information: How a didjeridu is made (see *Music and dance*, p.46).

Activities:
- Listen to tape of didjeridu music.
- Practise using clapping sticks to rhythm of music.
- Divide into groups, as in Lesson 2. Each group devises a dance or 'stamp' to represent its Dreamtime creature, as in *Music and dance*, p.46.

Lesson 8
Location: Hall.

Role of teacher: (a) Aboriginal.
(b) Mining engineer.
Costume: (a) As in Lesson 1.
(b) Hard hat, overalls.

Artefacts:
- Stones or large pebbles.
- Sand or sawdust.
- Clapping sticks (made in Lesson 2).
- Didjeridus (made in Lesson 2).

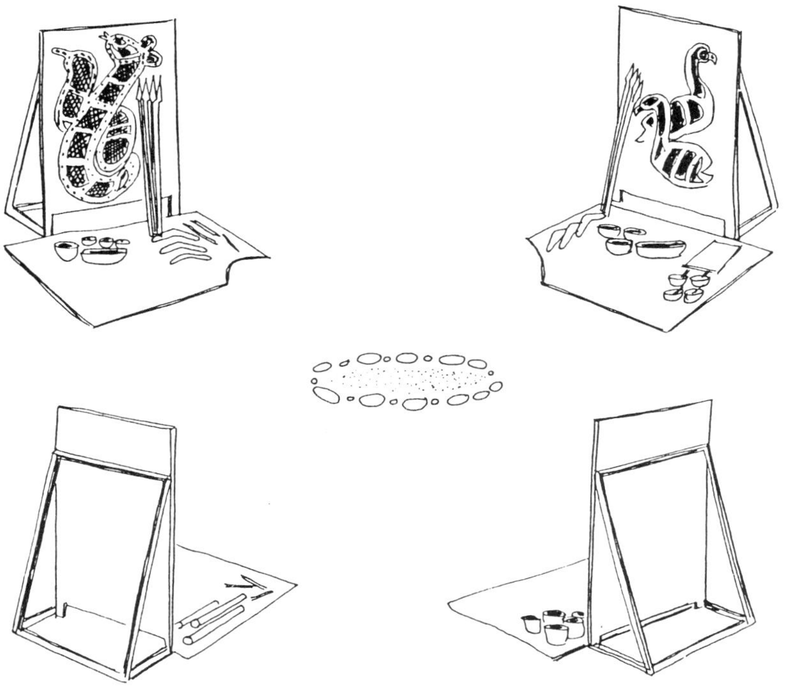

Setting: See illustration.

Theme: Celebration and land-rights.

Activities:

- Children go into hall and sit in four groups on mats in the corners.
- One group sends round message stick, as in Tiwi group work.
- Groups gather round the sand circle, bringing their mats which they arrange round the sand circle to form the Aboriginal flag. Teacher in role explains the flag p.55. Each group introduces itself in turn and the corroboree proceeds, as in Part C of programme.
- While the stamps are taking place, teacher changes role to become the Mining engineer. The interruption takes place, as on p.57.
- Teacher comes out of role and takes children back to classroom, where a discussion takes place, as in Part E, p.57.

Follow-up work, as for the *My Land* programme, could include an assemply showing some aspect of Aboriginal life to the rest of the school. Children could take on the various roles and use artefacts that were made during the lessons.

SEASONS of CHANGE
FLAIL
FLAT BLADED SHOVEL AND WOODEN RAKE
WIDE MESH RIDDLE
RIDDLED CORN
WINNOWING BASKET
THRESHING

SOLOMON ALLEN
SARAH HUGHES
MARTHA WERNHAM
HANNAH BURROUGHS
ABIGAIL THOMAS
CHILDRENS COSTUME
WERNHAM FAMILY
HUGHES FAMILY
BURROUGHS FAMILY
THOMAS FAMILY

Seasons of Change

Topic

The Topic for this programme is Agricultural Life in 1830.

Aim

The aim is to give children a broad understanding of how land enclosures and agrarian reform affected people in small villages.

Objectives

These are:

- to learn about family life in a farming community in 1830.
- to practise some of the household skills.
- to appreciate and practise some of the work that was done by children in and out of the home.
- to discover what village life was like before the enclosure of the land.
- to try out some of the farming methods that were used in the 1830s.
- to experience the effects of the Enclosure Acts on village people.
- to find out what happened to the villagers when farming began to be mechanized.

Research

If possible, visit a local museum of farming or rural life.

Books

Hobsbawm, E.J. and Rude, George (1969) *Captain Swing*, London: Lawrence & Wishart.
Horn, Pamela (1976) *Labouring Life in the Victorian Countryside*, Dublin: Gill & Macmillan.
Horn, Pamela (1974) *The Victorian Country Child*, Kineton: Roundwood.
Samuel, Raphael (ed.) (1975) *Village Life and Labour*, London: Routledge & Kegan Paul.
Shire Albums:

Agricultural Hand Tools (100), Ray Brigden 1985
Baskets and Basket-making (92), Alastair Heseltine 1982
Domestic Byegones (20), Jacqueline Fearn 1987
Shepherding Tools and Customs (23), Arthur Ingram 1983
Princes Risborough: Shire Publications.

Read:

- the pig-killing scene in *Jude the Obscure* by Thomas Hardy.
- the farming scenes in *Tess of the D'Urbervilles* by Thomas Hardy.

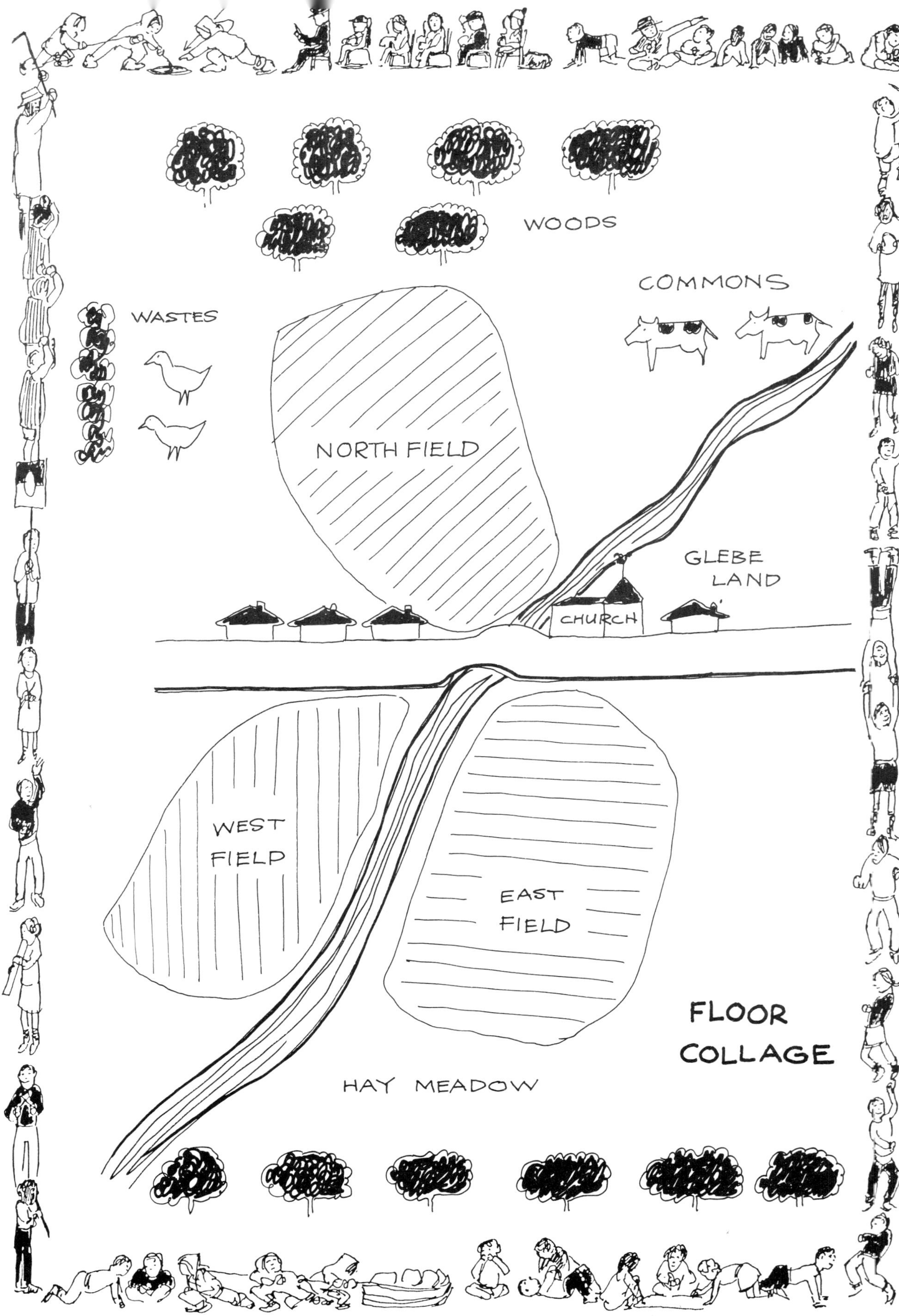

FLOOR COLLAGE

Outline scenario

The children will go back in time to 1830, when they will join the families of some of the villagers in a small village in Berkshire. They will take part in rural life and learn the reasons for the Swing Riots which took place in the 1830s.
The setting is the village of 'Kennetfield'.

Roles

There were five roles in the original programme:

Solomon Allen (Ploughman)
Sarah Hughes (Mother of village family)
Martha Wernham (As above)
Hannah Burroughs (As above)
Abigail Thomas (As above).

The programme may be done by three or four people by combining the roles.

If there are only one or two, use or adapt the Lesson plans (see p.87.

The programme in detail

The programme can be divided into six parts:
Part A The beginning
Part B Th Enclosures (large-group work)
Part C Cottage life (small-group work)
Part D Threshing (large-group work)
Part E 'Captain Swing' (large-group work)
Part F The ending.

Part A: The beginning
Location: Classroom.
Role of team member: Solomon Allen.
Scenario: Solomon Allen comes into classroom and introduces himself. The children put on sacking clothes and their name-labels. He tells the children that they are going back in time to the year 1830.

Information and discussion

- The difference between a village child's life in 1830 and today — no cars, television, radio, electricity; not many schools, none free, etc.

The children are taken to the hall to join their 'mothers'.

Part B: The Enclosures
Location: The rest of the programme takes place in the hall.

Setting: The village, represented by a collage laid on the floor. The cottages are in the four corners.

Roles:
- Solomon Allen/Government agent.
- Martha Wernham.

Kennetfield Inclosure

Notice is hereby given, that the Commissioner appointed in and by a certain Act of Parliament entitled 'An Act for Inclosing Lands in the Manor and Parish of Kennetfield in the County of Berkshire will meet at the House of William Daffran called the Falcon Inn in Theale in the County of Berkshire on Thursday 23rd day of August next at 11 o'clock in the forenoon when and where the several proprietors may attend and see the situation of their respective allotments. — Dated this 18th day of July 1810 —

By Order of the Commissioner.

John Richards

We, the villagers of Kennetfield demand the right to work and a living wage.
Also we demand that you Jacob Croker destroy your threshing machine within three days or we will not be able to answer to the consequences.

-Signed- Captain Swing

- Sarah Hughes.
- Abigail Thomas.
- Hannah Burroughs.

Scenario: 'Mothers' (Martha Wernham, Sarah Hughes, Abigail Thomas, Hannah Burroughs) collect their children and explain a little about their families and about the conditions at the time.

Solomon Allen enters, singing *The Poor Labourers*. The children join in the chorus.
Mothers explain to children what life was like ten years ago before the enclosures.

MARTHA WERNHAM
Lived in cottage on common. Gleaned corn left over after harvesting and made flour. Made own bread from flour. Grazed pig on waste land and in forest. Gathered firewood from forest. Grew vegetables in garden.

SARAH HUGHES
Owned three strips of land in each of the three fields. Those in Great field were given rent free by farmer because Sarah's husband saved his life one winter. Grew enough corn to bake bread throughout the year. Kept cow on common and pig in woods.

ABIGAIL THOMAS
Lived in cottage on common. Grew vegetables in 1/4-acre garden. Kept cow and geese, which grazed beside road and on waste land.

HANNAH BURROUGHS
Rented three strips of land. Able to grow two crops each year (one field left fallow each year to restore goodness). Right to graze cow on common.

All had the right to gather mushrooms, herbs, berries, firewood, etc. from forest and common, and to catch rabbits and hares in the fields and fish from the river.

Solomon talks about what happened ten years ago.
He puts on top hat and acts the role of the Government agent who, in 1820, was sent to enclose the fields. He reads out the Notice of Enclosure.

The Government agent then proceeds to question rights to strips, giving a small amount of land to those who can prove their right to it. He points out that those with land must hedge it at their own expense. He evicts cottagers from cottages on the common land, which now belongs to Farmer Croker. With the string he encloses the fields and points out that the villagers no longer have rights to the common land. Removes cow.

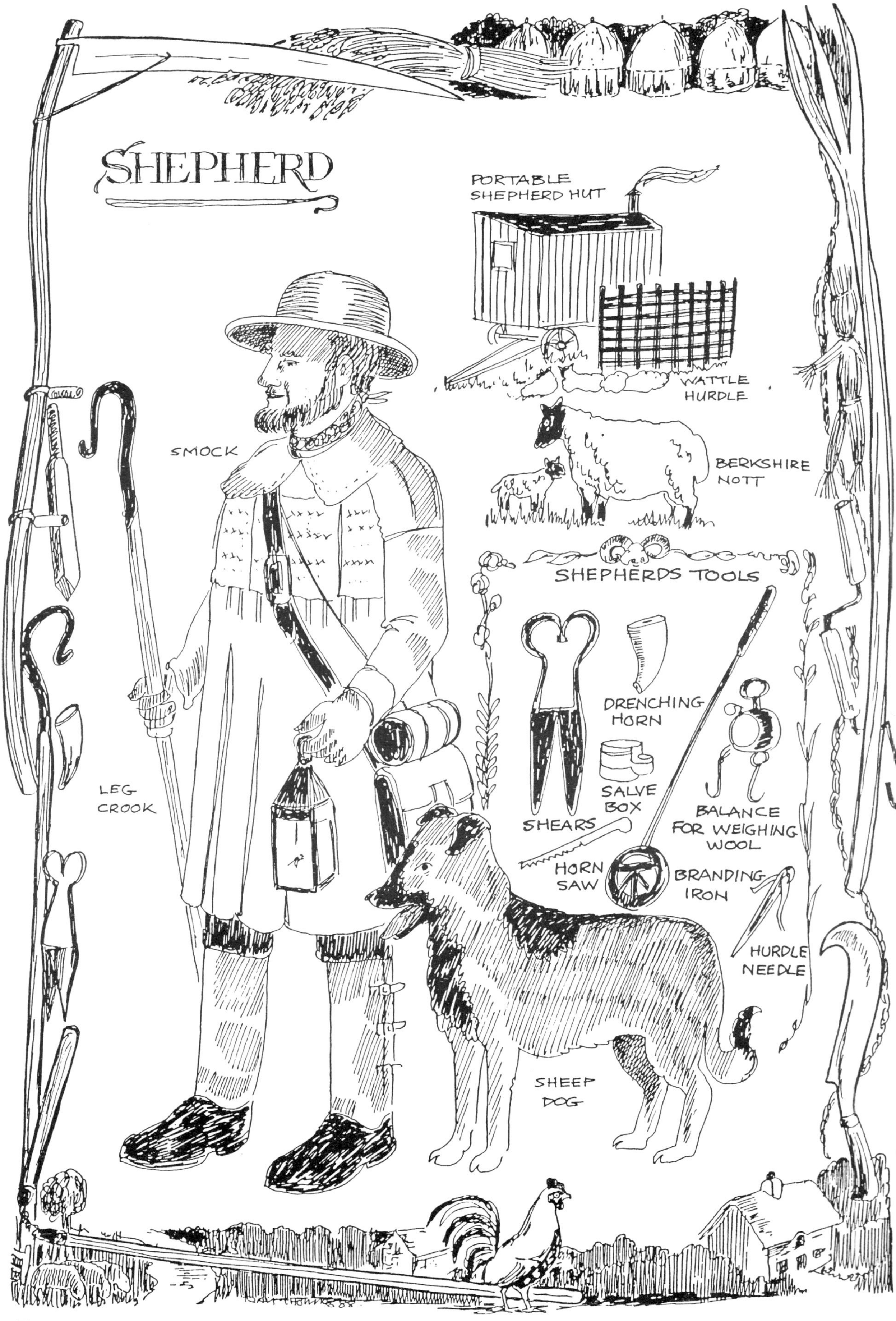
SHEPHERD
PORTABLE SHEPHERD HUT
WATTLE HURDLE
SMOCK
BERKSHIRE NOTT
SHEPHERDS TOOLS
DRENCHING HORN
SALVE BOX
SHEARS
BALANCE FOR WEIGHING WOOL
HORN SAW
BRANDING IRON
LEG CROOK
HURDLE NEEDLE
SHEEP DOG

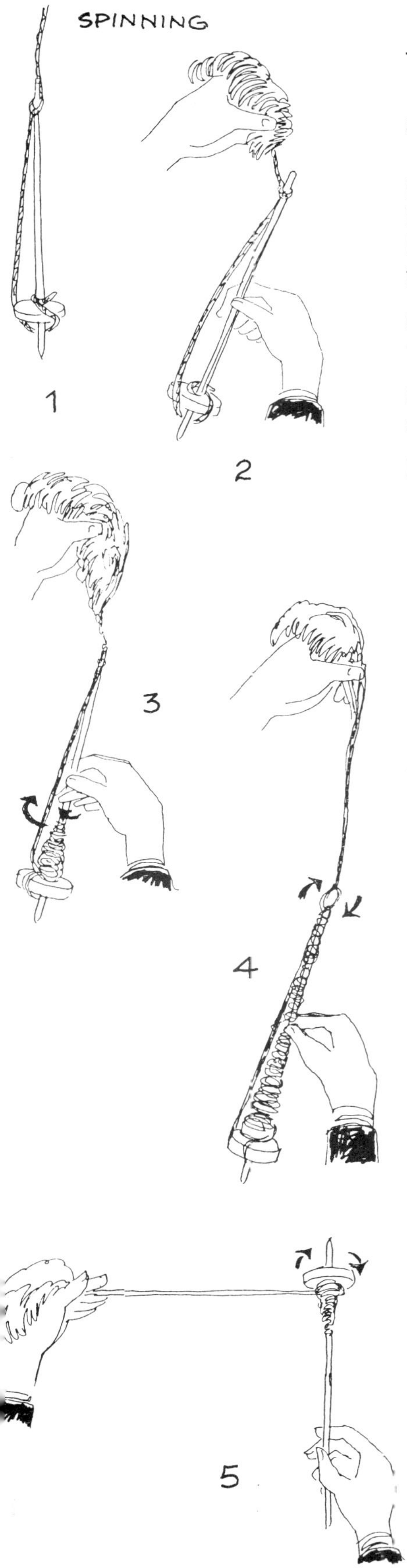

The children are taken by mothers to cottages.

Solomon removes the collage.

Part C: Cottage life
During this part, there is interaction between the families: borrowing household implements from each other, taking wool to be spun or dyed, exchanging news, etc.

Settings: Interiors of cottages.
1 Wernham Family

Scenario: Martha tells the children about her life before and after enclosure.

Family history:
- Husband is in prison for poaching a hare from what used to be the common land.
- Martha lives on parish benefit (enough money to buy two loaves a week for herself and each member of family).
- She owns a spinning wheel, which was her mother's, and earns some money by spinning wool for other people.
- Lives in cottage in village with small plot of land, where she grows vegetables for her family.

Learn rhyme

'They hang the man and flog the woman
That steals the goose from off the common
But leave the greater criminal loose
That steals the common from the goose.'

Information
- Where do the sheep graze? (Part of strip land enclosed during Tudor times now belongs to Manor.)
- How to find wool; how to clean it with soapwort.
- Martha spins wool for Sarah whose husband receives a fleece in part payment for his work. In return she keeps some of the wool.

Activities
- Teasing wool (drawing out the fibres).
- Carding.
- Spinning — either with wheel or with a spindle.
- Knitting squares to make into blankets.

Discussion
- What work could the children do to help out?

Activities
- Bird-scaring.
- Clearing stones from fields.
- Turnip cleaning.

HEDGER
MAUL
HEDGER'S TOOLS
HEDGE HOOK
HEAVY SKIN COAT
STONE SLIP FOR SHARPENING
SACKING APRON
DANNOCKS
SLASHER
BILLHOOK

CARDING

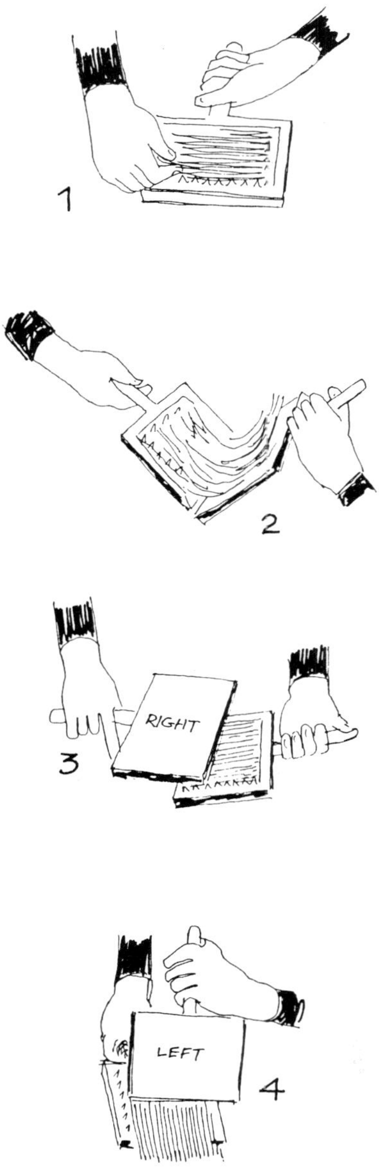

Learn bird-scaring rhyme

'Cadows and crows
Take care of your toes
For here come my clappers
To knock you down back'uds
Holla, ca-whoo, ca-whoo!'

Discussion

- What happens if you don't work hard? (Farmer could beat you and send you home without wages.)

2 Hughes Family

Scenario: Sarah offers the children whey, which was given to her by the dairyman. She tells the children about her life.
Family history:

- Husband is shepherd in regular employment.
- Weekly wage means that they are better off than most of their neighbours. They help when they can but life is hard for everyone.
- Strips exchanged for patch of poor marshy land. Had to sell some to pay for hedging and agent's fees. Still keeps a pig.

Information and discussion

- Who had the right to keep a cow on the common before enclosure?
- How to milk a cow, how to make cheese, churn butter.
- What the pig eats (acorns and snails).
- Pig killing: meat for the rest of the year.
- Land is very marshy, needs draining.

Activity

- Learn how to lay drain pipes, using shovel to dig the trenches. Pipe labelled DRAIN but Sarah cannot read.

Discussion

- Reading and writing.

Information

- This village, like many others, has no school. Where there are schools the children have to pay, so that most village people cannot read and write.

Sarah asks which two children would like to learn reading and writing from Solomon Allen. These children go to join Solomon's group, taking with them one or two from each of the other families.

Information and discussion

- Solomon is planning a meeting to protest about the lack of work and food. There are strict laws against such meetings. Should the Hughes family attend such a meeting?

Activity

- Making patchwork.

CARTER
FARM CART
HAMES
BUNKERS
BIT
COLLAR
BRASSES ON MARTINGALE
HAME
SHAFT
COLLAR
BRASSES TO WARD OFF THE EVIL EYE
VARIOUS TYPES OF HORSESHOES

Discussion

- Compare with outside jobs for children; bird scaring; stone picking; setting potatoes, peas and beans, etc.; harvest, haymaking, etc.

3 Burroughs Family

Scenario: Hannah talks about her life now and ten years ago. She asks one of the children to look after the 'baby' (Bessie).

Family history:

- Husband a carter: seasonal work helping with the horses at ploughing, harvest time, etc.
- Life difficult now that they have no land.
- Mother was village midwife.
- Hannah knows many plant and other remedies.
- Dyes wool and material for people in return for keeping some for herself.

Information and discussion

- Home remedies:

Dry throat — make a carrot concoction.
Whooping cough — eat a fried mouse.
Bruises — apply onion skin.
Cuts — apply elderflower ointment.
Corns — apply clove of garlic.
Warts — rub with snail (then bury the snail and as it rots so will the wart).
Arthritis — wear a potato next to the skin.

Activities

- Dyeing of cloth using fruit and vegetable dyes (blackberries for pink, lichen and moss for yellow and green, onion skin for yellow, etc.)
- Grinding herbs with pestle and mortar.

4 Thomas Family

Scenario: Abigail describes life in the past and now.

Family history:

- Abigail is a widow.
- When her husband died of consumption, she spent all of her savings on a decent funeral so that he would not be shamed by a pauper's funeral. The death bell tolled nine times for him. (It would toll six times for a woman and three for a child.)
- Her husband was a hedger, so did seasonal work.
- Never owned any strips of land but has a small plot of garden at back of cottage, where she grows vegetables.
- Used to live in a better cottage but was turned out when the land was enclosed.
- Receives benefit from Parish.

Discussion

- How she can earn some money.

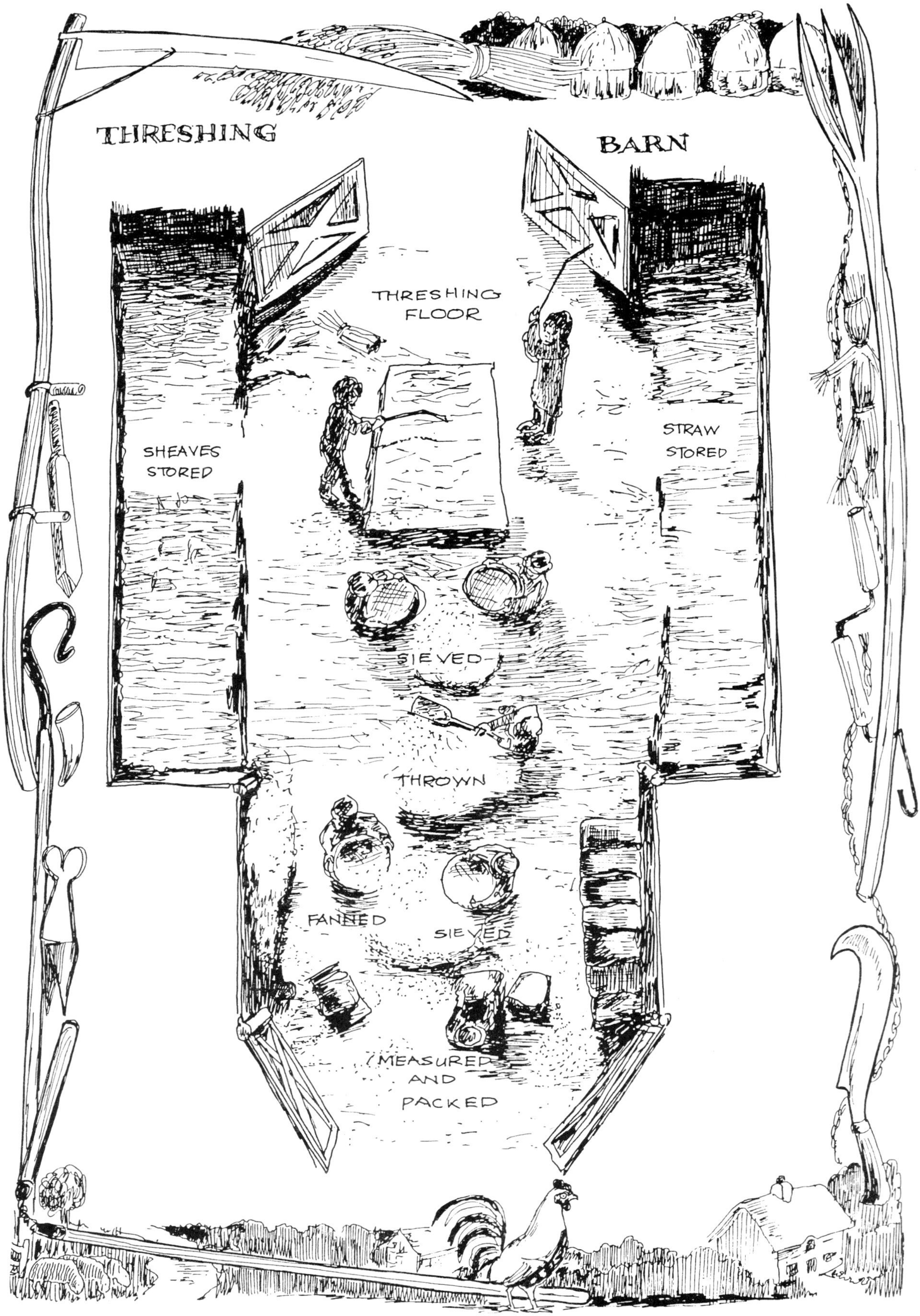
THRESHING
BARN
THRESHING
FLOOR
SHEAVES
STORED
STRAW
STORED
SIEVED
THROWN
FANNED
SIEVED
MEASURED
AND
PACKED

Activities
- Some of the children sent out bird-scaring.
- Some sent out to clear stones from the fields.
- Borrow the wash tub and dolly from Martha to do the washing.
- Straw plaiting (stitch plaits together to make hats).
- Collect withies from stream and make baskets.
- Make rag-rugs with rags collected from other groups.

5 Solomon Allen's group
as for 4. above

Scenario: The children go to Solomon to learn reading and writing.

History:
- Solomon is a ploughman.
- Works seasonally.
- Wages so low that he needs Parish benefit.

Information
- Using loaf of bread to explain how poor relief is calculated.

Activity
- Learning how to use breast plough and harrow.

Information and discussion
- The hiring fairs: insecurity of employment.
- Many of Solomon's friends have left the village. Some have emigrated, some travel to other villages looking for employment, some are in prison for poaching to keep their families alive, some have gone North looking for work in the mills.
- Solomon feels that something should be done to protest about the lack of work and low wages.
- He takes the children back to their cottages, talking to each family about the situation before he goes off to see if Farmer Croker has any threshing work.

Part D: Threshing

Setting: The threshing barn.
The team members move back the cottages and artefacts, leaving a large area of floor space.

Scenario: The families gather together to talk and exchange news and ideas.

Each family learns how the threshing is done and families learn their own activity: flailing, sieving, shovelling, winnowing, measuring and sacking. They practise the threshing song (*Country Hirings*).

Solomon returns with the news that there is threshing work in the old barn. They hurry to barn, divide into families, and start work. They must work hard in order to earn as much as possible.

Break for lunch. Bread shared out. Sing *The Women's Song*. Solomon goes to ask for a jug of ale from farmer. Returns with

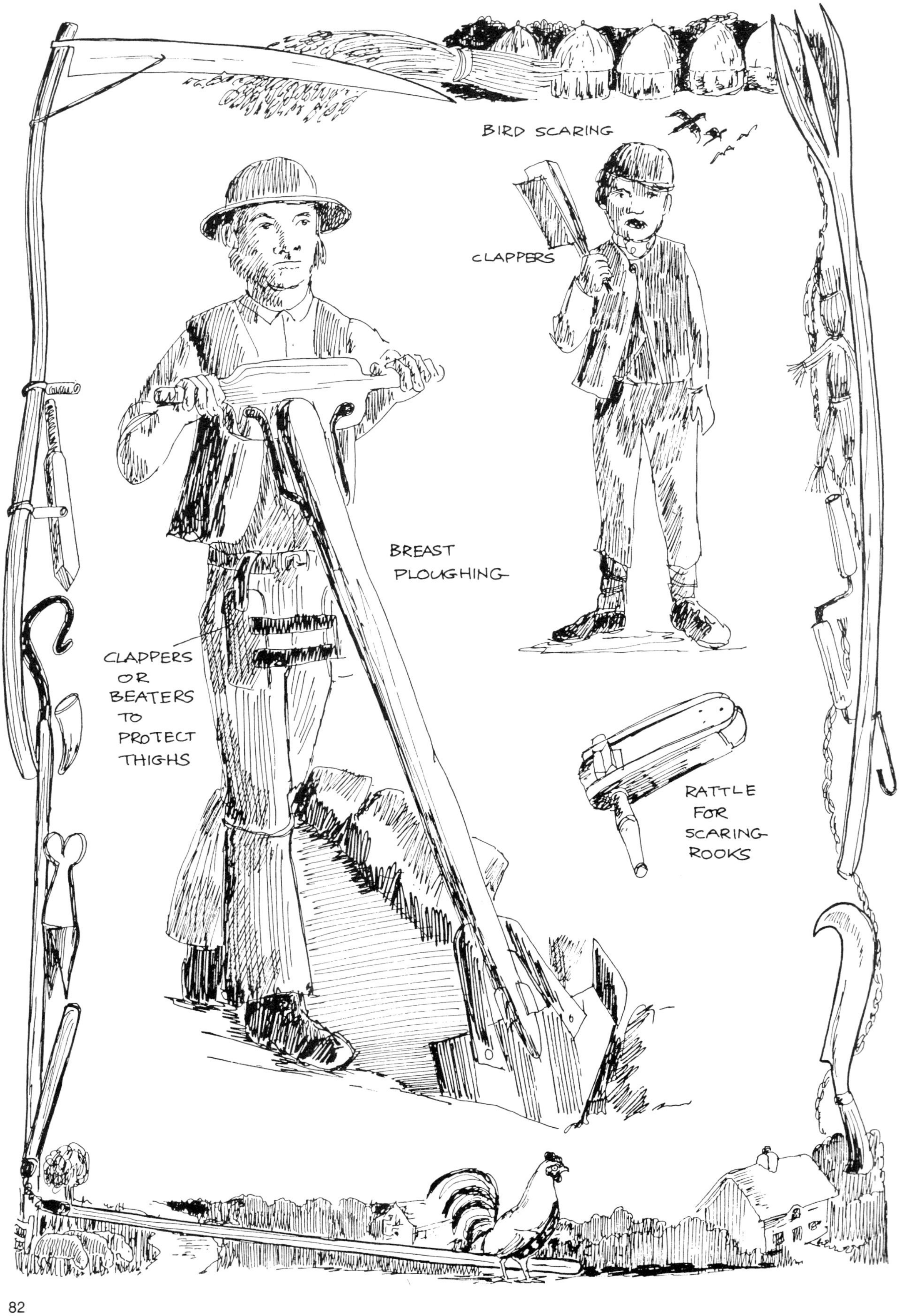
BIRD SCARING
CLAPPERS
BREAST PLOUGHING
CLAPPERS OR BEATERS TO PROTECT THIGHS
RATTLE FOR SCARING ROOKS

half a day's wages (not enough for a loaf of bread) and the news that the farmer's new threshing machine has arrived so there is no more work.

Part E: 'Captain Swing'

Scenario: All discuss what will happen now. Solomon suggests sending a letter to the farmer, demanding that he destroy the machine or else they will take action; the letter is to be signed by 'Captain Swing'.

Each family puts forward its views, the better off being against the letter and the poorer feeling that they have nothing to lose.

A vote is taken. Whatever the result, Solomon says that he will send the letter and leaves to do so, accompanied by all except one of the mothers.

Part F: The ending

The remaining teacher de-roles (by taking off hat or shawl). S/he then tells them what happened to the real Solomon Allen. He led a band of men who destroyed a threshing machine. Later he was charged with rioting and was transported to Van Diemen's Land (Tasmania).

The children take off their sacking clothes and discuss what they have experienced.

Follow-up work

The *Seasons of Change* Resource Pack contains many ideas for follow-up work.

- Discuss unemployment now and in 1830.
- Compare the introduction of machinery in 1830 with computerization today.
- Plan an assembly, which is researched by the children, depicting the life of Solomon Allen. The children, as villagers, give their points of view. Landowner explains why he needs a threshing machine, the vicar explains the poor payments' law. Interweave with songs and demonstration of threshing.
- Visit a farming or rural life museum in your area.

Some places to visit

Museum of English Rural Life
The University
Whiteknights
Reading
Berkshire
Tel.: 0734 875123, Ext. 475.

Butser Ancient Farm Project
Queen Elizabeth Country Park
Gravel Hill
Horndean

Hampshire
Tel.: 0705 598838

Hampshire Farm Museum
Manor Farm
Upper Hamble Country Park
Botley
Hampshire
Tel.: 04892 6305

Cogges Agricultural Museum
Church Lane
Cogges
Witney
Oxfordshire
Tel.: 0993 72602

Old Kiln Agricultural Heritage Museum
Reeds Road
Tilford
Farnham
Surrey
Tel.: 025125 2300

The Great Barn
Avebury
Wiltshire
Tel.: 06723 333

Practical organization

Costume

The women should wear long dresses of rough material, sacking aprons, shawls, straw hats, boots.
If possible, the man should wear a smock or rough trousers, old collarless shirt, and sleeveless jerkin. Boots.
Ask children (if possible) to bring an old sack or piece of rough material to wear during the programme. (Do not tell them why they need it.)

Settings

- The village green.
- Four cottages.

Artefacts, materials, and equipment

The following list includes the artefacts that were used by the Learning Through Action team but it may be reduced if items are unavailable.

Local farming or rural life museums may be helpful in lending some items or providing pictures as a substitute.

Ask local people to help.
The children can make the floor collage and the cottage backgrounds

Preliminary work
- large piece of material (old sheet).
- material for collage.
- card, scissors, paint, etc.
- large pieces of corrugated card (for 'cottages').

Part A
- name-labels for children.

Part B
- large floor collage to represent the village.
- top hat.
- ball of string.
- cut-out cow and geese.
- strips of material to represent strips of land.
- Notice of Enclosure.

Part C
Wernham Family:
- screen painted to show poor cottage, doused fire, cooking pots, a few dried herbs and vegetables.
- stool.
- spinning wheel or spindles if possible (if you can borrow these, ask the owner to show you how to use them).
- carders and wool fleece (may be obtained from someone who spins; ask around).
- knitting needles and wool.

Hughes Family:
- screen painted to show more comfortable home; tools of shepherd's trade shown; dairy implements.
- milking stool.
- slates and chalk.
- jug of 'whey'.
- drainage shovel (if not obtainable, use any large shovel).
- piece of old drain pipe labelled DRAIN.
- bird clappers.
- wash dolly and tub, scrubbing board, washing line, and pegs; either borrow or improvise).
- material, needles, and thread for patchwork.
- loaf of brown bread.

Burroughs Family
- screen painted to show carter's tools; also dried herbs and plants for remedies.
- wash dolly and tub.
- pestle and mortar.
- herbs.
- dyeing bowl and water.
- onion, carrot juice.
- lichen, moss, blackberries or other berries.
- salt and salt box.
- large doll wrapped in rough shawl.

Thomas Family
- screen painted to show poor background; some hedger's tools.
- withies for basket making.
- straw for plaiting.
- rushes for rush-light making.
- rags for rug-making.
- large needles and cotton.
- acorns.

Solomon Allen
- breast plough (see illustration).
- beaters
- harrow
- loaf of brown bread.

Part D
- flail.
- large sieve.
- shovel.
- winnowing basket (any large flat basket).
- bread.

Part E
- letter.

Practical and preliminary work
Organize one or more practical sessions with the children. Do not tell them about the programme. This is most important.
1 Collage of village before the enclosures showing:
- common land.
- woodland.
- wasteland.
- fields divided into strips.
- cottages.
- river.

This can be made of paper or material.
2 In groups, paint background to cottages.
3 Paint inn sign (the Jolly Farmer).
4 Cut out twelve strips of material to represent strips of land.
5 Cut out paper or cardboard cow and geese.

Ask children to bring in any scraps of material which could be used for patchwork and rug-making.

Collect or make other artefacts. Large items, such as the breast plough and drainage shovel, can sometimes be borrowed from local rural life museums. If this is not possible, improvise or find large photographs or drawings to show the children what they were like.

Before programme
Teach children the choruses of the songs.

Divide the children into family groups. Give them labels with their family name and ask them to add their own first name.

Make sure that each child has a sacking garment.

Set up hall as for My Land.

Lesson plans

These are for the teacher who is working alone or with one colleague.
Much of the information required is contained in the description of the programme above and reference is made to the various parts of the programme.

Lesson 1
Practical and preliminary work: As in programme.

Lesson 2

Location: Classroom and hall.
Setting: The hall should be set up beforehand with village collage in centre (see p.70).
Role of teacher: Solomon Allen.

Costume: Try to find some items of clothing to suggest the role (see p.84). This need not be elaborate.
Role of Children for Lessons 2-8: Village children from 1830.

Costume for children: If possible, each child should wear a piece of sacking or rough material.

Artefacts, (see programme for details):
- Collage of village.
- Cut-out cow and geese.
- Strips of material.
- Notice of Enclosure.
- Ball of string.
- Top hat.

Base lesson on Parts A and B of programme.

Separate children into four family groups by labelling them with the four family names (Wernham, Hughes, Thomas and Burroughs).

Explain that they will be going back in time to 1830, as in Part A of programme.

Take children to hall.

Explain the circumstances of each family in turn, as in Part B of programme.

Put on Government agent's top hat and carry out enclosure of the land, as in programme.

Children sit in circle in their families, teacher in role as Solomon Allen. Discuss the consequences of enclosure. How will families survive? Some will have to poach and steal, some will move away to towns, some will become tied labourers for the landowner on a small wage.

Lessons 3, 4, 5, 6
Role of teacher: Each of the four mothers in turn.
Base lessons on Part C. These could be reduced to three lessons but be sure to include both poor and the most well-off families.
If there are two of you, divide the class into two families.
If you are single-handed, divide the class and work between the groups, setting an activity to be carried out in one family while talking to the other.

Wernham Family (for example)

Role of teacher: Martha Wernham.

Setting: Cottage, as described on p.75.

Artefacts: As listed on p.85.
Information, discussion, and activities: As on pp.75-77.

Lesson 7

Location: Hall

Role of teacher: Solomon Allen.

Artefacts:
- Breast plough.
- Beaters.

Borrow both of these from museum, or improvise.

- Loaf of bread.

Base lesson on Solomon Allen's group, p.71.

End with Solomon going to Farmer Croker to see if there is any work.

Lesson 8

Location: Hall
Role of teacher: Solomon Allen.

Artefacts:
- Flail.

- Large sieve.
- Shovel.
- Winnowing basket.
- Bread.
- Letter.

If it is not possible to obtain any of these, this section could be carried out using improvisation.

Base lesson on Parts D and E, Threshing and 'Captain Swing'. Learn threshing activities, all together at first then each family takes on one part (see p.81).
Practise song (*Country Hirings*).
Continue as in Parts D and E of programme.
Finish as for programme. Solomon takes off hat and tells children what happened to the real Solomon Allen (see p. 83).
End with discussion (all out of role).

Follow-up work
As for programme.

A WOMAN'S WORK IS NEVER DONE

Come all around both old and young and listen to my song,
I'll tell you of a circumstance that would not keep you long.
I saw a man the other day as savage as a Turk,
And he was grumbling at his wife and said she did not work.

CHORUS: So men if you would happy be,
Don't grumble at your wife so,
For no man can(t) imagine,
What a woman has to do.

He said "You lazy hussy, indeed you must confess,
For I'm a tired of keeping you in all your idle mess".
But the woman she made him answer saying "I work as hard as you.
Then I will just run through the list what a woman has to do".

CHORUS: So men if you would happy be, etc

At six o'clock each morning off to work ye de go,
There's eight to rise and light the fire and the bellows for to blow.
I have to set the tea things and get the kettle boiled,
Besides you know I have to work and dress the youngest child.

CHORUS: So men if you would happy be, etc

Tis four times a day, a once for to employ,
His breakfast, dinner, tea and supper we have to stew and dry.
I have to shake and make the bed and sweep the rooms all so,
I have to dust the windows and empty the chamber po.

CHORUS: So men if you would happy be,
Don't grumble at your wife so.
But think on your poor mother,
How she put up with you.

A WOMAN'S WORK IS NEVER DONE

THE POOR LABOURERS

You sons of old England, now list to my rhymes,
And I'll sing unto you a short sketch of the times,
Concerning poor labourers you all must allow,
Who work all the day at the tail of the plough.
CHORUS: O, the poor labourers, pity poor labourers,
That are working for five or six shillings per week.

There's many poor labourers to work they will go,
Either hedging or ditching to plough or to sow,
And many poor fellows are used like a Turk,
They do not get paid for half a day's work.

CHORUS: O, the poor labourers, etc

And many poor labourers I'm sorry to say
Are breaking of stones for eightpence a day;
Bread and water's the fare of the poor labouring man,
While the rich they can live on the fat of the land.

CHORUS: O, the poor labourers, etc

Some pity the farmers, but I tell you now,
Pity poor labourers that follow the plough,
Pity poor children half starving and then,
Divide every great farm into ten.

CHORUS: O, the poor labourers, etc

There are many young fellows you'll see every day,
For snaring a hare they are banished away,
To Van Diemen's land or to some foreign shore,
And their wives and children are left to deplore.

CHORUS: O, the poor labourers, etc

THE POOR LABOURERS

COUNTRY HIRINGS

Come all you blooming country lads and listen unto me,
And if I do but tell the truth I know you will agree.
It's of the jolly farmers who servants want to have,
For to maintain them in their pride and be to them a slave.
CHORUS: Servant men stand up for wages,
When to the hirings you do go,
For you must work all sorts of weather,
Both in cold, wet and snow.

The farmer and his wife in bed so snug and warm can lie,
While you must face the weather, both cold, wet and dry;
For the rates they are heavy, and the taxes they are high,
And we must pull the wages down, the farmers they do cry.

CHORUS: Servant men stand up, etc

The farmers twenty years ago could their rents and taxes pay,
But now they are so full of pride, it increases every day;
Which makes the landlords raise the rent, and the farmers for to scold,
On the poor young servant lad, and rob him of his gold.

CHORUS: Servant men stand up, etc

The farmer and the servants together used to dine,
But now they're in the parlour with their pudding, beef and wine,
The master and the mistress, their sons and daughters all alone,
And they will eat the meat, and you may pick the bone.

CHORUS: Servant men stand up, etc

The description of your living, I'm sure it is the worst,
For the pottage it is thin and the bread is very coarse,
While the masters they do live, as you shall understand,
On butter and good cheese and the fat from off the land.

CHORUS: Servant men stand up, etc

COUNTRY HIRINGS

OPERATION HIDEAWAY
RP
EBS
EBS
Ray Thomas 89
THE EVACUEES

JOYCE TURNER
(TEACHER)
NURSE JAMES
(SCHOOL NURSE)
CAPTAIN
JOHNSTONE
(RETIRED ARMY
OFFICER ALSO
A MEMBER OF
THE HOME GUARD)
PAUL STEWART
(BILLETING OFFICER
AND AIR RAID
WARDEN
CARYL EVANS
(LANDGIRL)
RULES

Operation Hideaway: The Evacuees

Topic

The title of the programme is *Operation Hideaway*, the name given to the mass evacuation of children from London and other high-risk areas to safer parts of the country during the Second World War. This particular programme deals with the evacuation of children from the Paddington area of London to Reading, but children in many city areas had similar experiences.

Aim

To give the children an experience of a major world event which changed the way of life of everyone in this country and which is still within the memory of many grandparents and older people.

Objectives

These are:

- to learn about conditions in England in 1939-40.
- to find out how some Londoners were living at this time, looking in particular at a small area of London.
- to give the children the chance to experience what it might have been like to be an evacuee in 1940.
- to learn about some of the problems and difficulties which were encountered.
- to compare the lifestyle of a child during the Second World War with that of a child in the 1980s.
- to give children an opportunity to practise some of the skills that were considered necessary in addition to school work at the time.
- to gain some understanding of how change comes about and what are the consequences of change.
- to foster links between children and the older generation by learning something about the events that older people experienced when young.

Research

People

Many grandparents and older friends have memories of the war years as well as mementoes which they might be willing to lend.

Special material

Imperial War Museum,
Lambeth Road
London SE1 6HZ
Tel: 01 735 8922
Very helpful especially for visual material.
Library and college archives.

GAS MASK
GAS MASK CASE
RATION BOOK
IDENTITY CARD
RATION BOOK FOR FOOD
TELEPHONE
". . . but for heaven
don't say I told
CARELESS
COSTS
". . . strictly between
these four walls!"
CARELESS TALK
COSTS LIVES
PICTURE POST
Lilliput

Schools in areas where evacuation took place may have records or log books giving information.

Books

Allen, E. (1975) *Wartime Children 1939-1940*, London: A. & C. Black

Fyson, N.L. (1981) *Growing up in the Second World War*, London: Batsford.

Grant, I. & Maddren, N. (1975) *The Countryside at War*, London: Jupiter.

Keeping, C. (1975) *Cockney Ding Dong*, London: Penguin.

Sellman, R.R. (1964) *The Second World War*, London: Methuen.

Snellgrove, L.E. (1970) *World War II*, Harlow: Longman.

Tapes

The Second World War (One of a series, *Six of the Past*), from Learning Through Action Centre, Cumberland Road, Reading, Berkshire.

English with a dialect (BBC cassette) from BBC Enterprises, Woodlands, 80 Wood Lane, London W12 0TT (Tel.: 01 743 5588)

Cockney speech, from British Dialects,

Sound effects, from Mike McMillan, Bulmershe College, Reading University, Reading, Berkshire (Tel.:0734 663387).

Outline scenario

The outline scenario is that the children will go back in time to 1940 and, as children from Seaton Street School in Paddington, will take part in the evacuation of children from London to Reading. They will be lodged with different families in Reading and attend the local school.

Roles

There are five roles:

- Joyce Turner (Teacher)
- Nurse James (School Nurse)
- Captain Johnstone (Retired Army Officer and member of Home Guard)
- Paul Stewart (Billeting Officer and Air Raid Warden)
- Caryl Evans (Landgirl).

If there are three or four team members, double up the roles. If there are only two or if you are working on your own, adapt the programme and use it as the basis of a series of lessons to be presented on consecutive days or over a number of weeks (see Lesson plans, p.106).

A 1930's LIVING ROOM

The programme in detail

This is preceded by 3 preliminary sessions in class (see Practical organization p.103).

The programme can be divided into six parts:

Part A The beginning
Part B The journey (large-group work)
Part C Inspection and billeting (large-group work)
Part D Settling into new homes (small-group work)
Part E School (large-group work)
Part F The ending.

Part A: The beginning

Location: Classroom.

Role of team member: Miss Turner.

Scenario: Children occupied with finishing off posters. Miss Turner enters classroom.
She introduces herself as a new teacher from the country. She assumes that the school is Seaton Street in London. She asks the children about London, the Blitz, etc.
The children take on the roles that they have developed previously. They talk about their lives and families as children of Seaton Street School. They show Miss Turner their gas masks and sing the songs that they have learned.
They are interrupted by a knock at the door. A telegram is handed in. This tells the new teacher that serious air-raids are about to begin and that it is important to take the children immediately to a place of safety.
They collect their belongings, gas masks, identity cards, blankets, etc. and are told to sit quietly in their places.
The atmosphere should be very serious.
Children are given labels on which they write their name and which they are told to wear at all times.
They are told never to go out of doors without carrying their gas masks.

Part B: The journey

The children are taken to cloakroom to collect coats.
While they are out of the room, the rest of the team set up chairs in the classroom to represent a coach.
One of the team may play the coach driver.
The children come back, get into 'coach' and begin the drive to their new home.
Miss Turner moves around asking how the children feel about leaving London, what they can see out of the window, what they think their parents may be thinking, etc. (In the original programme, the children were taken in a real, blacked-out coach to a hall in a different building and really did not know where they were going.)

DANCING
TO THE
BARREL
ORGAN
IN SEATON STREET
PADDINGTON
ARP

Part C: Inspection and billeting

Location: Hall.

Setting: 'Homes' set out in four corners. In the centre of the hall is the Billeting Officer's table, on which is a list of the children's names and a note of the family to which they will be allocated.

Roles:
- Miss Turner.
- Mr Stewart.
- Nurse James.
- Captain Johnstone.
- Caryl Evans.

Scenario: The coach arrives at its destination.
The children are taken into hall.
The children are met by Mr Stewart
They are told to be quiet and line up to be examined by Nurse James. She tells them to stand in bowl of 'disinfectant' and she searches their heads for lice.
When children have been seen by Nurse James, they are allocated to their new homes by Mr Stewart. There may be some problems about splitting up families and friends.

Part D: Settling into new homes

1 Nurse James' home
- Nurse James is efficient but kind and motherly.
- She is very welcoming.
- Home is warm and cosy.
- She understands that the children are homesick and encourages them to talk about their homes and parents.
- She gives them Ovaltine and biscuits before tucking them up in their blankets for night.

2 Captain Johnstone's home
- Captain Johnstone is a retired Army officer.
- He is pompous and authoritarian.
- Lives alone.
- No comforts, sparse furnishings.
- List of rules.
- Children must wash in cold water.
- They make their own beds and go to bed without anything to eat or drink.

3 Mr Stewart's home
- Mr Stewart is an Air Raid Warden.
- Rejected for military service.
- Not unkind but not welcoming.
- Tells children about blackout.
- Gives them a lecture about their behaviour.
- Allows them to try on his Warden's helmet.
- Takes prayers before children go to bed.

4 Caryl Evans' home

- Caryl is a landgirl, pleased at being able to help the war effort by working.
- Home is cheerful (rug on floor, pretty tablecloth, flowers in vase, etc.).
- She loves her work and enjoys the open air.
- She is understanding with the children as she too is a long way from home.
- Produces paper and pencils so that children can write home.
- Helps children to get ready for bed, hot water to wash in.
- Children given cocoa.

Scenario: All children settle down for night. Listen to radio ('Uncle Mac' story) before lights are put out.
Lights on again.
Morning sounds.
All improvise dressing, having breakfast.

Part E: School

Scenario: Miss Turner collects children from their homes and takes them to school (either in another room in the school or in part of the hall set out with benches). War posters and 'times tables' displayed but otherwise stark and uninteresting.
Miss Turner explains that they will be at school only for the morning, as the local children will be there in the afternoon.
Miss Turner gives an arithmetic lesson in 1940's style.
She explains that in order to save paper they will use slates to write on.
She then explains that the children must learn other skills.
Nurse James gives First Aid lesson. All learn sling making.
Mr Stewart talks about air raid precautions and carries out gas mask drill.
Caryl Evans talks about farming and tells the children how to pick up potatoes (which is what they will do during the afternoon).
Captain Johnstone gives P.T. lesson (exercises and drill).
Miss Turner takes children back to their host families.

Part F: Time ending

The hosts and the children de-role (perhaps by taking off an item of clothing, or by removing gas mask cases). This is a time of calming down and coming back to the 'real world'.

Discussion

- How life continued for evacuees. Some went back to the city, some stayed for the duration of the war.
- The effects of the war on the evacuees.
- What the children thought about the experience.

Follow-up work

1 Tape a discussion about the people whom the children met and about their attitudes.

2 Collect news items, stories, and artefacts from grandparents and older friends. Arrange a display and make a scrap-book.
3 Produce a class newspaper.

Stimulus
- Papers and newspapers from the period.

Content
- Articles about the evacuees and their parents.
- News items.
- Pictures.
- Advertisements.
- Propaganda.
- Jokes.
- Letters.

4 Organize an assembly to show to the rest of the school 'life in 1940'. This could include role play, grandparents' memories, reading out of newspaper items, songs, etc.

Practical organization

Costume
Nurse's uniform for Nurse James.
Air raid helmet for Mr Stewart.
Home Guard cap for Captain Johnstone.
Other characters try to find items of costume to suggest the style of the 1940s. Drama wardrobes may be able to help. Ask if grandparents have anything suitable in their attics.
Children may also be asked to find an item of clothing which suggests the period and to bring this in on the day of the programme.

Settings
- Billeting hall.
- Four 'homes'.
- School.

Artefacts, materials, and equipment
Most of these will be easy to obtain. Suggestions are made for finding the more specialized items.
For preliminary work
- pictures of the period (from *Picture Post* or old newspapers).
- slides of London in 1939-40.
- projector and screen.
- examples of advertisements from the time (may be obtainable from local paper or libraries).
- examples of Second World War posters.
- recording about London Blitz
- tape recording of cockney speech

- Card, scissors, string, yoghurt cartons, coverfilm, glue, Sellotape, paper reinforcements etc. For making gas masks and identity cards
- labels

Part A
- gas masks and identity cards (made in preliminary session).

Part B
- chairs to simulate coach.

Part C
- table
- bowl of water (for 'disinfecting' feet).
- height pole.
- scales.
- list of children's names and names of billeting families.

Part D
- furnishings for homes (according to type of home): tables, chairs, rugs, mugs, vase of flowers, list of rules, old radio, etc. These can be simple or more elaborate according to availability.
- paper and pencils.
- tape recorder.
- recording of 'Uncle Mac' type story (a children's story of the period read by a man in style of 1940s).
- recording of morning sounds.

Part E
- board and chalk.
- benches.
- map of world.
- propaganda posters (may be obtainable from local libraries or Imperial War Museum).
- slates and chalk.
- triangular bandages.

Preliminary work

Organize three sessions with the children a few days before the programme. Do not tell the children what will happen during the programme. This is most important.

Session 1

Introduction
- Slides and pictures of scenes in Britain before the outbreak of the Second World War:
  street games.
  street scenes.
  cinema.
  dance halls.
  schools.
  factories.

Stimulus
- Recording about the Blitz.

Information and discussion
- Historical background to Second World War.

- First World War: 'war to end all wars', trench warfare, Armistice, Remembrance day, poppies, etc.
- Hitler: power in Germany, hatred of Jews, marching into neighbouring countries, Poland, declaration of war, 'phoney war', Britain alone.

Discussion
- Rationing.
- Clothing.
- 'The war effort'.
- Social life.
- Air raid shelters.

Session 2
Each child given individual case book containing revelant information: fact sheet, case history page, space for personal details and design.

Fact sheet
- Memories of Seaton Street.

The 'Ding-Dong' man came round on his bicycle selling icecream bricks: 4d for a whole block, 2d for half.
Milk came from a large churn. People brought their own jugs or containers to be filled.

On the sweet stall the sweet man twisted his own cough-candy and cut pieces off with scissors. There was a large cauldron full of sticky toffee mixture. The children brought their own apples to dip in to make toffee apples.

If the family was short of money the mothers would go to the Pawn Shop to pawn their belongings. They would pawn anything from sheets to their wedding rings. They would collect them on Friday when they were paid.

The children always had holes in their shoes. They would put cardboard in the shoes to fill the holes.

A girl's ambition was to have black patent leather shoes with ankle straps. Some children put bottle-tops on their shoes to make taps.

If the girls had an argument they would settle it by staring each other out. They stared at each other until one looked away and lost the battle.

Sometimes the children would sit on the steps outside a shop telling ghost stories. Sometimes they frightened each other so much that they were afraid to go home and would shout for their mothers to come and get them.

Activity
- Children start to built up individual characters of a child from Seaton Street School in 1940. They may work alone or with one 'brother' or 'sister'. Their characters should be of the same age or older than themselves.

Writing
- In case book, write section of diary or autobiography, bringing in information about family, home, hobbies, etc. and how the war has affected them.

Research
- What were clothes like?
- design clothes for character

Stimulus
- Tape of cockney speech.
- Fact sheet.

Improvisations (in small groups)
- Street scene: street vendors selling from barrows; playing games; street songs, etc.

Session 3
Activities
- Make gas masks and cases.
- Make identity cards.

Discussion
- Dangers of war.
- Subject of evacuation.

Stimulus
- Propaganda posters from Second World War.

Discussion
- Propaganda, what it is, how it works

Activity
- Design propaganda posters.

Discussion
- Morale and what it means.

Learn songs

Pack up your troubles,
Hey little hen,
Maybe it's because I'm a Londoner, etc.

On the day before
- Ask children to bring their item of 1940s clothing and a rug or blanket, rolled up and tied with string.

On the day
- Set up billeting area and 'homes' in hall before programme begins.
- Decide where 'school' will be and set it up.

Lesson plans

These are for the teacher who is working alone or with one colleague.

Most of the information required is detailed in the programme above.

Lesson 1

Location: Classroom.
Materials and equipment:

- Projector and screen.
- Slides (or pictures if projector not available) showing scenes in Britain at the beginning of the Second World War.
- Recording about the Blitz (from Imperial War Museum or library).
- Advertisements from the period (from library or local newspaper archives).
- Illustrations of propaganda posters.

Base lesson on Session 1 of the preliminary work (historical background), p.104.

Lesson 2

Location: Classroom.

Materials and equipment:

- Tape recording of cockney speech (for address see p.97).
- Case book for each child, as detailed on p.106.

Base the lesson on Session 2 of the preliminary work.

Lesson 3

Location: Classroom.

Materials and equipment:

- Sugar paper, card, scissors, string, yoghurt cartons, coverfilm, glue, Sellotape, paper reinforcements, etc.

This lesson is mainly practical work (making gas masks, identity cards, propaganda posters), based on Session 3 of preliminary work.

Lesson 4

Location: Classroom and hall.

Setting: Hall set out as billeting hall.

Role of teacher: Miss Turner.

Costume: Suggestion of 1940's dress.
Artefacts, materials, and equipment:

- Gas masks, gas mask cases, and identity cards (made in Lesson 3).
- Bowl of water ('disinfectant').
- Table.
- List of names of children.
- Posters started in Lesson 3.

At the start of the lesson, the children should be finishing their practical work on posters.

Change to take on the role of Miss Turner, who arrives from the country and assumes that the school is Seaton Street in London. The children will take on the roles practised in a previous lesson. The lesson proceeds, as in Parts A and B and the start of Part C of the programme.

If you are working with a colleague, s/he can set out the chairs to represent the coach while the children are in the cloakroom collecting coats. If you are working alone, the children can set out the chairs to make the coach in the classroom.

The final destination is the school hall, where inspection of the children takes place.

If working alone, change to the role of Nurse James.

Lesson 5

Location: Hall.

Setting: Hall laid out as for Part D of programme.
Role of teacher:
(a) Nurse James.
(b) Captain Johnstone.
(c) Mr Stewart.
(d) Caryl Evans.

Costume: Some items of costume for each role, as in the programme. This need not be elaborate but just enough to suggest the character.

If there are two of you, each can take on two of the host roles, changing roles between your two homes.

If you are working on your own, start with the following extra work:

Divide class into four groups. Each group is given a description of a different household with which they will be billeted. Build up the character of the host or hostess by asking the children questions about the character (age, family, home, interests, friends, attitudes to evacuees, etc.). In groups, improvise scenes where hosts meet in the street and talk about the possibility of evacuees coming to stay. Information about the different hosts is on pp.101-102

Later, during the lesson, one child in each group can take on the role of the host or hostess while the teacher moves from group to group in role as Miss Turner.

Take children to hall.

In role as Mr Stewart, allocate the children to the four homes, as at end of Part C of programme.

Base the lesson on Part D of programme, ending with listening to the 'Uncle Mac' story and 'going to sleep for the night'.

Lesson 6

Location: Hall

Setting: Rows of benches, etc., as for Part E of programme.

Role of teacher:
(a) Miss Turner.
(b) Mr Stewart.
(c) Caryl Evans.
(d) Nurse James.
(e) Captain Johnstone.

Base lesson on Part E of programme.

Teacher takes on roles in turn to take different lessons. (If two teachers, take two or three roles each.)

Finish off this lesson with de-roling and discussion.

Follow-up work
As for programme.

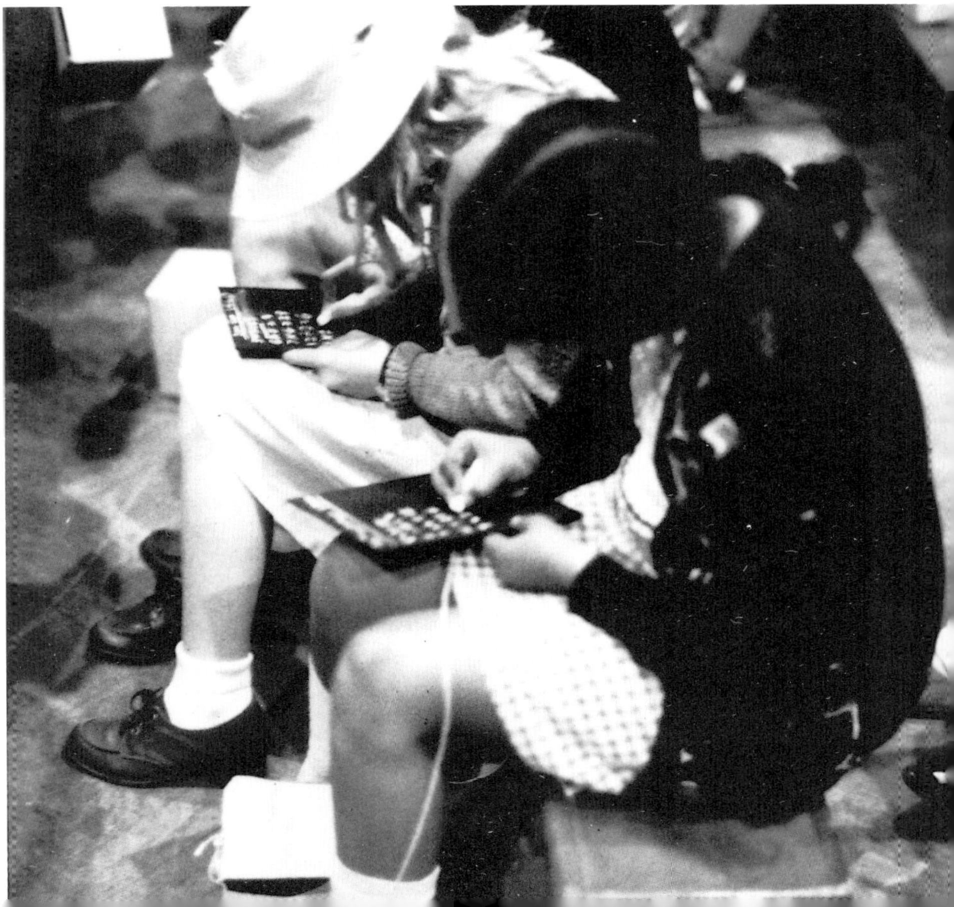

ANIMAL WATCH
Ray Thomas 89

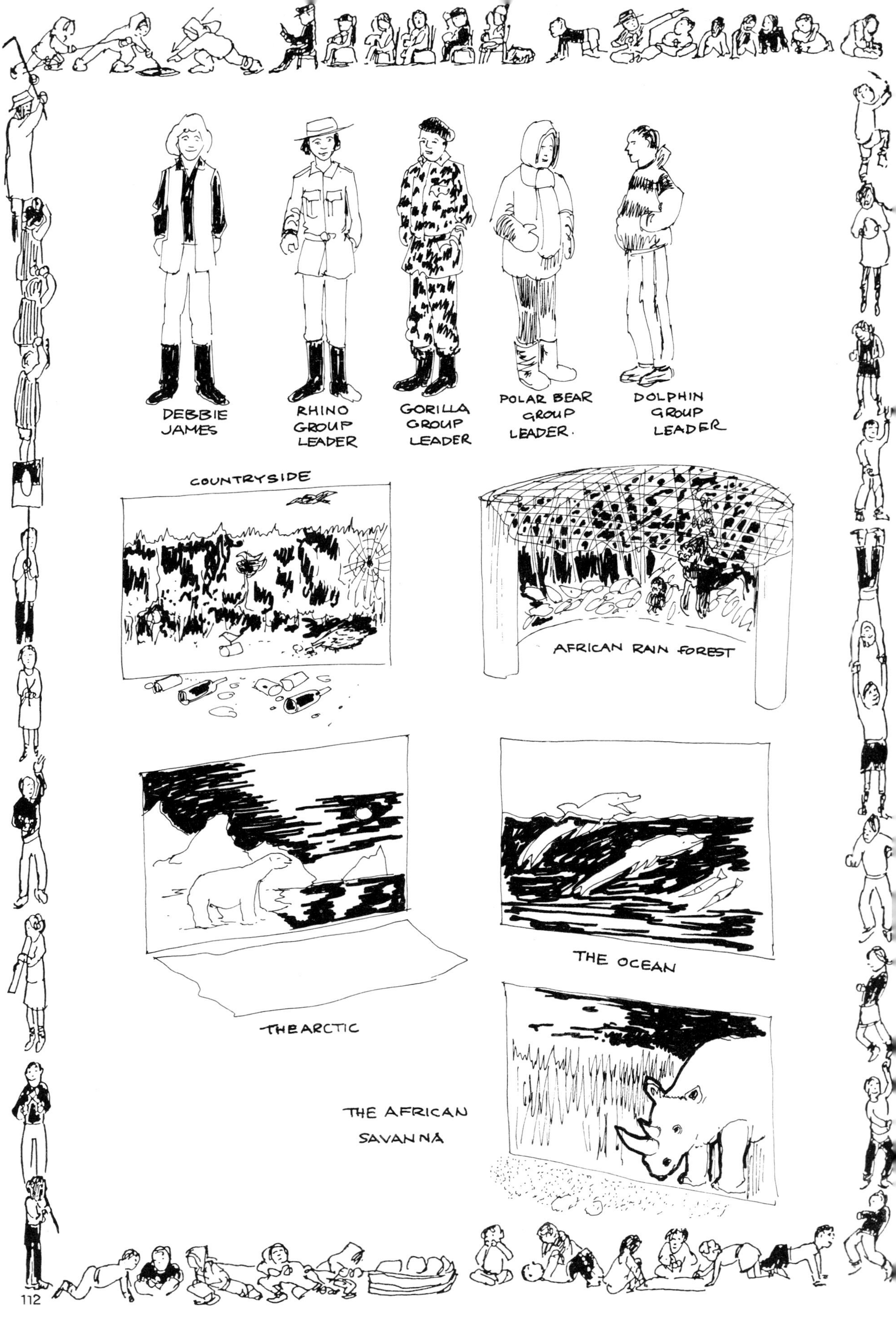
DEBBIE JAMES
RHINO GROUP LEADER
GORILLA GROUP LEADER
POLAR BEAR GROUP LEADER.
DOLPHIN GROUP LEADER
COUNTRYSIDE
AFRICAN RAIN FOREST
THEARCTIC
THE OCEAN
THE AFRICAN SAVANNA

Animal Watch

Topic

The topic is Animals in Captivity.

Aim

The aim is to look at the reasons for keeping animals in captivity and to question whether it is necessary or desirable. It is also to encourage an interest in animals: in their care and in consideration for their needs.

Objectives

These are:

- to compare the ways of life of animals in the wild and in captivity.
- to look at specific habitats, showing how they differ from each other and how in some areas they are in danger of being destroyed.
- to pose the question, 'should animals be kept in captivity?'
- to encourage thought about how conditions might be improved for animals in captivity.
- to look at the relationship between people and environment.
- to raise questions of conservation and the need for policies which take note of problems of pollution and the destruction of habitats.
- to find out about extinction and endangered species and what can be done to help.
- to learn that, in the interest of animals, different environmental groups must be prepared to co-operate with each other.

Research

Useful addresses

The Conservation Trust
c/o George Palmer School
Northumberland Avenue
Reading
Berkshire
Tel.: 0734 868442

Council for Environmental Education
University of Reading
London Road
Reading
Berkshire
Tel.: 0734 875234, Ext. 218.

Friends of the Earth Trust Ltd
26-28 Underwood Street
London N1 7JQ
Tel.: 01 490 1555

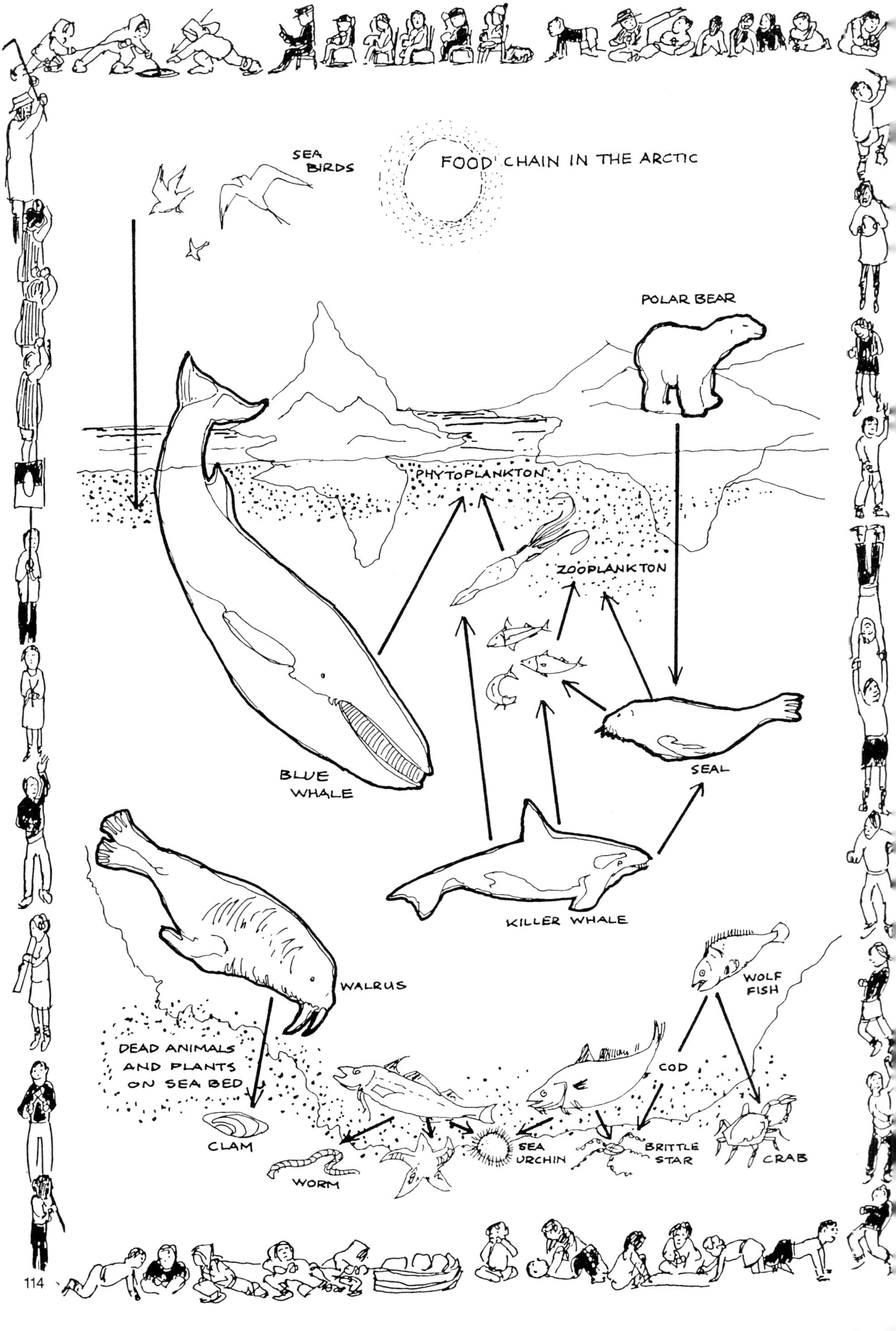
FOOD CHAIN IN THE ARCTIC
SEA BIRDS
POLAR BEAR
PHYTOPLANKTON
ZOOPLANKTON
BLUE WHALE
SEAL
KILLER WHALE
WALRUS
WOLF FISH
DEAD ANIMALS AND PLANTS ON SEA BED
COD
CLAM
WORM
SEA URCHIN
BRITTLE STAR
CRAB

RSPCA
Causeway
Horsham
W. Sussex RH12 1HG
Tel.: 0403 64181

Information on 'Operation Stronghold' and other conservation schemes from:

World Wide Fund for Nature
Panda House
Weyside Park
Godalming
Surrey GU7 1XR
Tel.: 04834 26444

Zoo Check
Cherry Tree Cottage
Cold Harbour
Nr Dorking
Surrey RH5 6HA
Tel.: 0306 712091

Books

Berry, Jim (1985) *Worldwise*, Godalming, Surrey: World Wildlife Fund.

Durrell, Lee (1986) *State of the Ark*, London: Bodley Head. (Information on endangered animals)

Fossey, Dian (1989) *Gorillas in the Mist*, London: Penguin.

King, Peter (1986) *Protect Our Planet*, London: Quiller/World Wildlife Fund.

Lockey, Ronald M. (1979) *Whales, Dolphins and Porpoises*, Newton Abbot: David & Charles.

Miles, Hugh and Salisbury, Mike (1985) *Kingdom of the Ice Bear*, London: BBC Publications.

Sackett, Russell (1983) *Edge of the Sea* (*Planet Earth* series), London: Time-Life Books.

Stonehouse, Bernard (1981) *Saving the Animals*, London: Weidenfeld & Nicholson/World Wide Fund for Nature.

Whipple, A.B.C. (1984) *Restless Oceans* (*Planet Earth* series), London: Time-Life Books.

Magazines

The Natural World
RSNC, The Green, Nettleham, Lincs LN2 NR

World Wide Magazine
World Wide Fund for Nature, Panda House, Weyside Park, Godalming, Surrey GU7 1XR.

Videos

(Obtainable from W.H. Smith and most video outlets.)

Bloody Ivory (National Geographic)

OTTER

RHINO

POLAR
BEAR

DOLPHIN

GORILLA

Gorilla (National Geographic)
Kingdom of the Ice Bear (BBC)
Polar Bear Alert (National Geographic)
Rainforest (National Geographic)
Zimbabwe (Horizon)

Outline scenario

The outline scenario is that an animal lover has died, leaving a sum of money to be used to benefit animals. The children will be taken to different habitats to learn about animals in the wild. They will then be asked to design schemes for using the money to the best advantage of the animals.
The settings for the first part of the programme will be five habitats; for the second part, the areas that need to be created or improved.

Roles

There are nine roles in *Animal Watch*. The programme can be done with a team of three, four, or five.

For a team of five:
a) Debbie James.
Leader of Otter group.
Controversial characters in part D.
b) Leader of Gorilla group.
Leader of gorilla design group.
c) Leader of Polar Bear group.
Leader of education bus design group.
d) Leader of Dolphin group.
Leader of wildlife park design group.
e) Leader of Rhino group.
Leader of zoo design group.

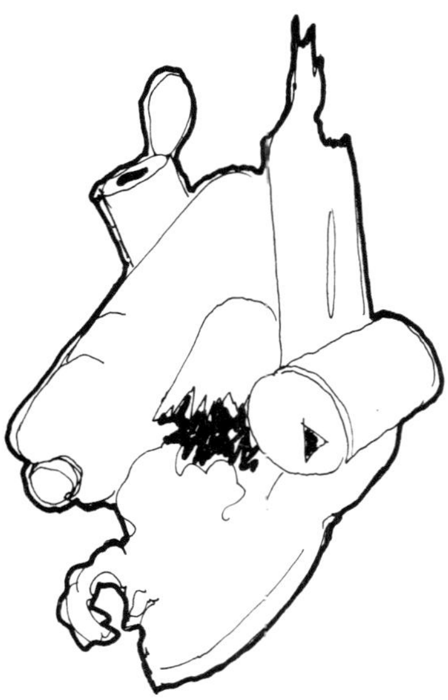

For a group of four:
Leave out one of the Habitat groups.
In Design section, each team leader leaves groups temporarily to take on a 'controversial character' role, visiting another group.

For a group of three, or if you are on your own or have only one colleague, you can either adapt the programme or use the lesson plans (see p.131) on consecutive days or at intervals of a few days.

The programme in detail

The programme can be divided into six parts:
Part A The beginning
Part B Habitats (small-group work)
Part C Sharing information (large-group work)
Part D Design (small-group work)
Part E The meeting (large-group work)

Part F The ending.

Part A: The beginning

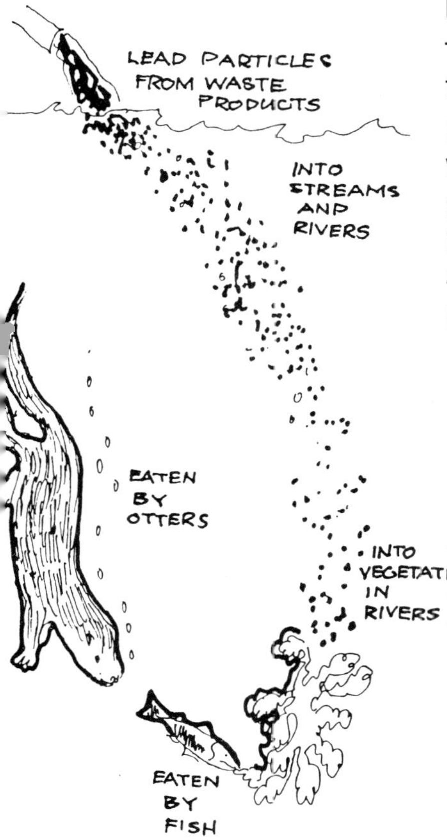

Location: Classroom.

The children are given colour-coded badges, placing them in four different groups for design part of programme.

Role of team member: Debbie James, a conservationist working with indigenous animals.

Scenario: Debbie comes into classroom. She introduces herself as a conservationist and asks if the children are the Animal Watch volunteers.

She tells the children that:

- her grandmother has left money in her will to be used to help in the conservation of animals.
- she would like the children to help with the carrying out of her grandmother's wishes.
- they should talk first to some animal experts to find out what are the needs of various animals.

She takes children to the hall.

Part B: Habitats

The children divide into animal groups and find their correct habitat.

Group 1
Emblem: Otter.
Habitat: Countryside.
Setting: Cardboard screen painted to show a hedgerow. The ground beside the hedgerow is covered with litter.
Role of team member: Conservationist, as in Part 1.
Scenario: The children visit the countryside with the conservationist to find out about the problems for the wildlife there.

Discussion

- Litter and its danger to wildlife. Why do people drop litter? What sorts of litter do they drop? What effect can litter have on animals?

Activities

- Collecting litter.
- Demonstration by team member of carrot in tin can, showing potential hazard for animals and human beings. This should be carried out very carefully, emphasizing the dangers.

Discussion

- How could tin cans be made safer?
- Destruction of the environment with the resulting danger to wildlife.

Activities

- Looking at bird's nest, observing, feeling, etc.

- Work on footprints, identification, making casts of hand-prints.

Discussion
- Dangers from people, snaring of animals.

Stimulus
- Photograph of fox family, photograph of dead (snared) fox.

Demonstration
- Snare and how it works.
- Fishing line and hooks: danger to swans and other water birds of entanglement or swallowing. Lead weights and danger of poisoning when swallowed by birds.

Information
- Accumulation of lead in otters through food chain.

Discussion
- The otter as an endangered species and the reasons for this. What can be done about it?

Group 2
Emblem: Gorilla
Habitat: African rainforest.
Setting: Cardboard screen painted to show rainforest, covered with netting and vegetation to give atmosphere.

Role of team member: A researcher who is studying a group of gorillas.

Scenario: The children accompany the researcher on a visit to a group of gorillas in the rainforest.

Stimulus
- Map of world.

Information
- Rainforests: world distribution, structure, inhabitants, (see *State of the Ark*).
- Destruction of rainforests and reasons for this. (Need for mineral mining, more land for farming, timber, roads, etc.)
- Tropical climate, reasons for differences in world climates, in animals and vegetation, in lifestyles.
- Endangered species, and reasons for this (destruction of habitats, poaching).
- Poaching.

Discussion
- Who does the poaching? Who organizes it? Why does it happen? What can be done about it?

Demonstration
- Snares and how they work.

Activity
- Finding and studying a group of gorillas: tracking techniques, approaching the group, body language, grooming, vocalization, feeding (see *Gorillas in the Mist*).

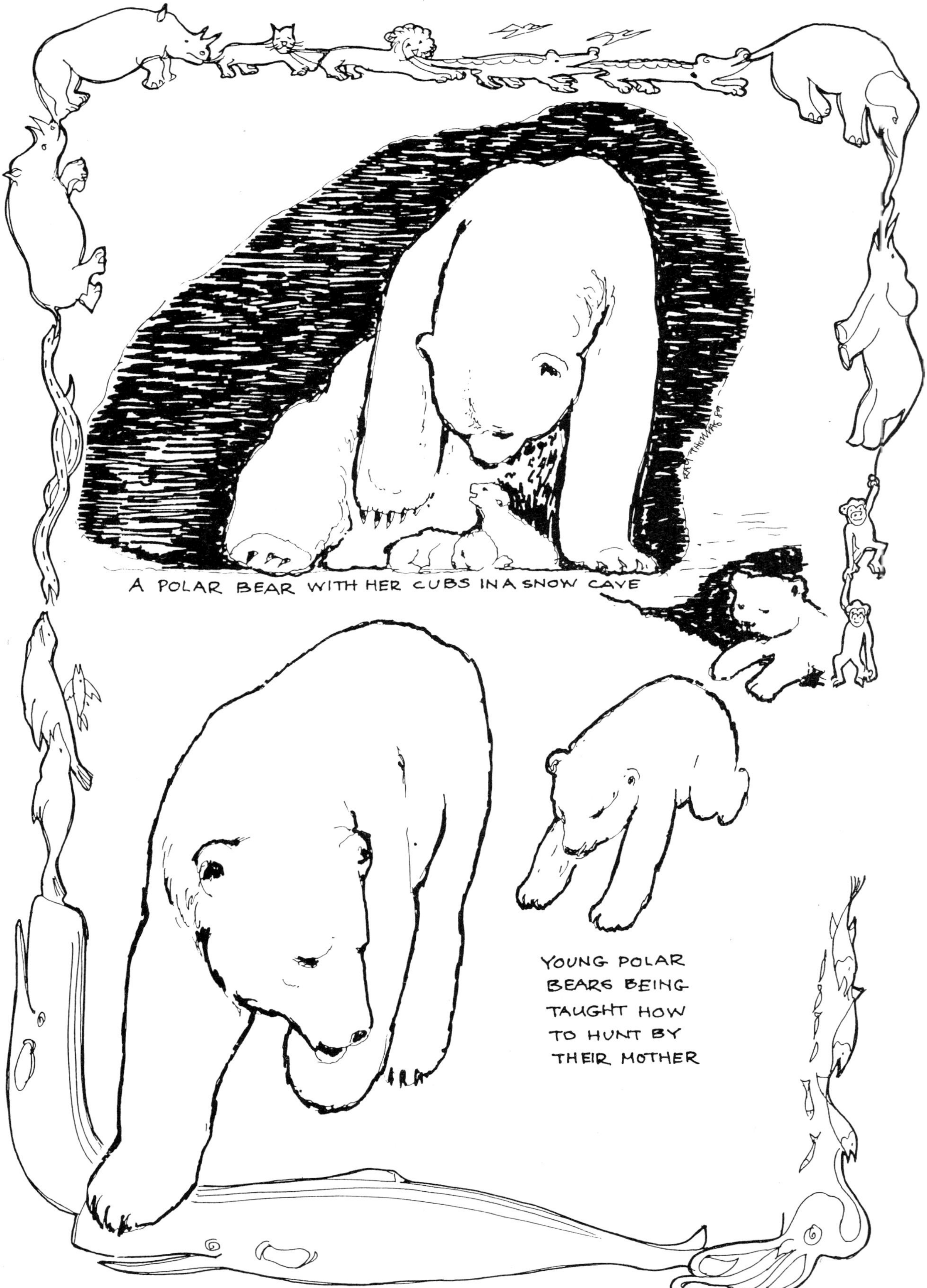

A POLAR BEAR WITH HER CUBS IN A SNOW CAVE

YOUNG POLAR BEARS BEING TAUGHT HOW TO HUNT BY THEIR MOTHER

Discussion

- Gorillas in zoos. How does their lifestyle compare with life in the wild? Why are they kept in zoos?

Group 3
Emblem: Polar Bear.
Habitat: The Arctic.
Setting: Cardboard screen painted with Arctic scene. Sheet representing snowy ground.
Role of team member: Arctic naturalist, studying polar bears and other Arctic creatures.
Scenario: The children are asked to help in a polar bear survey, monitoring the movement of the animals and spotting any dangers.

Stimulus

- Globe of the earth.

Information

- Location of the Arctic. Reason for the cold climate.

Activity

- Using a torch to show the cause of night and day, summer and winter.

Information and discussion

- Animals of the Arctic and how they have adapted to the conditions (colour, fur, layers of fat, etc.).

Stimulus

- Equipment, rations, compass, etc.

Information and discussion

- Cold and the dangers of the Arctic, the need to be properly equipped.

Activities

- Learning to use binoculars and telescope. Spotting polar bears and other creatures.

Information

- Problems of and dangers to polar bears.
- Lifestyle and habits of polar bears, (see *Kingdom of the Ice Bear*).

Activity

- 'Denning' expedition, exploring a vacant den. Observe claw marks where female dug out the ice. When leaving, children slide out as bears would.

Discussion

- The Inuit (people of the Arctic): how they copied the polar bear in catching seals and how they now limit their killing of polar bears in order to keep them from becoming extinct.

Group 4
Emblem: Dolphin
Habitat: The Ocean.
Setting: Screen painted with ocean scene.

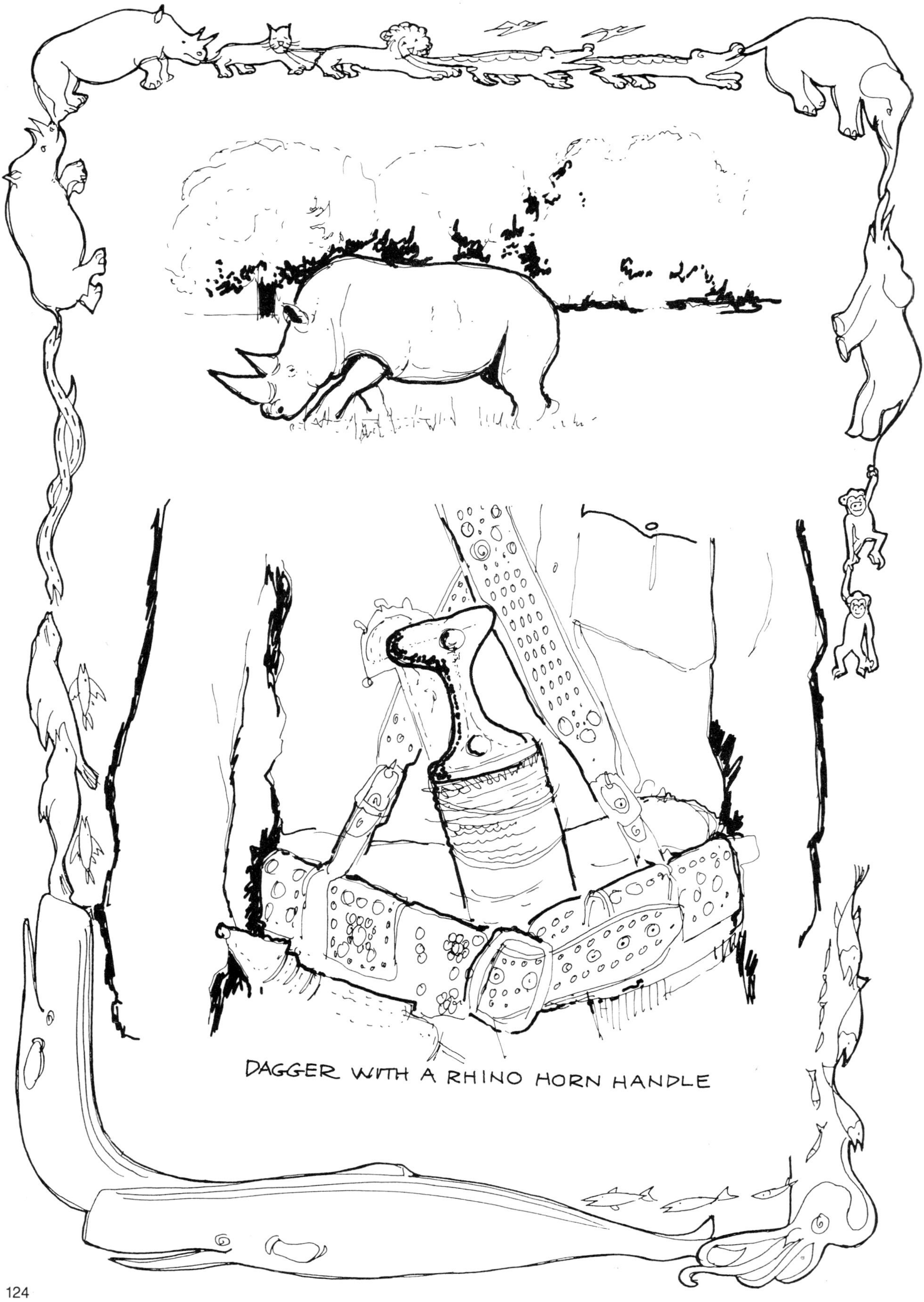

DAGGER WITH A RHINO HORN HANDLE

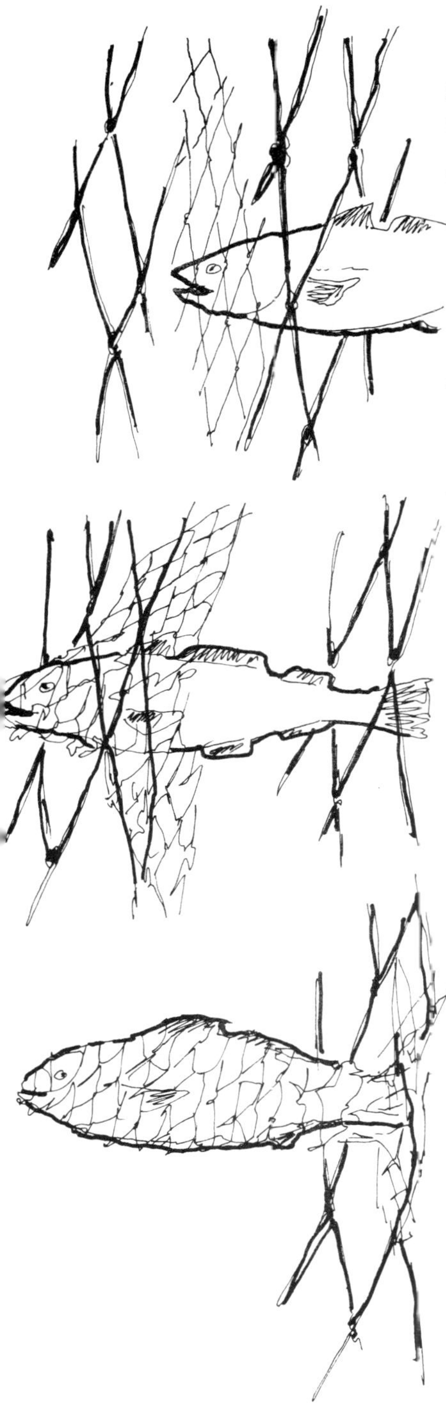

Role of team member: Marine biologist/diver.
Sub-roles:
(a) RSPB expert.
(b) Skipper of oil tanker.

Scenario: The children visit a marine research centre and go on a diving expedition.

Information and discussion
- Wild life of the ocean.
- Pollution and the consequent problems, including dumping of rubbish and other materials, oil spillage, use of toxic materials in ships (see *The State of the Ark*).
- Problems of tankers and spillage of oil.

Information
- Team member in role puts the point of view of the skipper of an oil tanker.

Activity
- Cleaning oil off feathers, showing the danger to sea-birds from oil pollution.

Information
- Team member in role puts the point of view of a member of the RSPB.

Discussion
- Problems caused by fishing, over-fishing, monofilament gill-nets anchored to the bottom of the sea.

Activity
- Demonstration of monofilament gill-net.

Discussion
- The problem of balancing the need for improving fishing methods with the danger to other sea creatures.

Activities
- Making of food chains.
- Techniques of diving: dependence on each other, sign language.

Group 5
Emblem: Rhino.
Habitat: African savanna.
Setting: Screen of cardboard painted to show savanna. On the floor, close by, footmarks have been made by scattering ash and treading in it.

Role of team member: Leader of rhino-saving team.
Sub-roles:
(a) Member of anti-poaching team.
(b) K'tunga, a poacher.
(c) A 'middle-man' in the poaching business.

Scenario: The children join a team, 'Operation Stronghold', who help to save rhinos from poachers by taking the rhinos to a safer area.

Stimulus
- Photographs of rhino.

Discussion
- Endangered species, especially the black rhino.
- Poaching and why it takes place.
- Poaching of elephants for the tusks (ivory).
- Problems for local people, such as lack of money, drought, flooding, hunting tradition.

Stimulus
- Announcement on 'walkie-talkie' that a group of poachers has been sighted, which the group must investigate.

Activities
- Tracking techniques (start with footprints on floor).
- Use of compass.

Information
- 'Operation Stronghold' and how it is helping to save the black rhino (information from Zoo Check).

Story-telling
- Much of the work in this group consists of story-telling by the teacher, in role, who puts the different points of view of various characters (see 'A Poacher's Story' from *Worldwise*).

Part C: Sharing information

Groups come together and:
- share information acquired.
- discuss animals in different habitats and whether they need protection.

Scenario: Debbie James explains that the children are now going to design four places which will be used for or help in the protection of animals. The best design will be awarded the money from the will. The first priority in judging the designs will be how the needs of the animals are catered for.

Group W
Project: A zoo that needs improvement.
Role of team member: Zookeeper.

Issues:
- Should zoos exist in their present form?
- How can they be improved?
- Breeding programmes for rare species.
- Does re-introduction of animals into the wild succeed?

Group X
Project: A single-species sanctuary for gorillas.
Role of team member: Ex-zookeeper.

Issues:
- Destruction of rainforest.
- Extinction of different species.

- Exploitation of animals (especially using apes and monkeys as entertainment).

Group Y
Project: A patch of undeveloped land to be used as a nature reserve for indigenous species.
Role of team member: Conservationist.

Issues:
- Reasons for otters being endangered (hunting for fur or for sport in the past, pollution, land drainage, loss of habitats through building, etc.).
- Problems of wild animals in this country (cutting down of hedgerows, destruction of habitats, pesticides, pollution, etc.).

Group Z
Project: A bus to be used as a mobile education centre, providing a base for the *Save the Rhino* campaign.
Role of team member: Education officer.

Issues:
- Poaching.
- Destruction of habitats in other countries (mining, building, over-cultivation, farming).
- Need to tell people what is happening to animals in Africa.

Part D: Design
Children are sorted into colour groups. (These are arranged to ensure that some from each habitat group are in each colour group.)

Setting: The screens are reversed, showing a background to the area to be designed.

Activity
- Children start designing their model.

Team Leader stays in background, advising when asked, but encouraging the children to use their own ideas from the information that they acquired during Part B.

As the children work, they can discuss the issues that are relevant to their design area. The team leader should ensure that all sides of an argument are clearly put to the children.

Scenario: While the children are working, they are visited by the first team member, playing a different role for each group. All of these characters are controversial and try to introduce ideas which conflict with the welfare of the animals.

Suggestions
Group W: A 'fun-ride' should be built through the middle of the zoo, using up much of the space needed for increasing the size of the cages and enclosures.
Group X: The gorillas should be taught to perform tricks.

Group Y: A boating lake should be made in the nature reserve.
Group Z: Video games about shooting wild animals should be shown.

The children are allowed to argue with this character as they think fit.

Part E: The meeting
When the models are completed, the groups assemble for a formal meeting, displaying their models in the centre of the hall.

Each group introduces its ideas and puts forward a case for being awarded the money which was left in the will.
General discussion led by Debbie James between all groups, including the team leaders. All points of view are put forward fairly and debated.

Debbie James decides that all of the designs are so good that the money will be divided equally among them. Since this means less money for the schemes, the children are asked to suggest fund-raising ideas. (This can be continued in follow-up work.)

Team leaders leave to meet the solicitors.

Part F: The ending
The team member playing Debbie James 'de-roles'. She talks to the children about the programme and what they have learned.

She asks them what ideas they have about helping animals both in the wild and in captivity; for example, writing to the RSPCA, to newspapers, to children's programmes or nature programmes on television or radio, if they encounter cases such as badly run zoos or cruelty to animals.

Follow-up work
- Writing letters as suggested in the programme.
- More detailed work on animals and habitats.
- A visit to a local wildlife park.
- A visit to a local zoo or animal sanctuary.

Take note of the conditions and the comfort of the animals. If these are not satisfactory, write to Zoo Check.

Some places to visit
The Monkey Sanctuary
Near Looe
Cornwall
Tel.: 05036 2532

The Sea-life Centre
Lodmoor Country Park

Weymouth
Dorset
Tel.: 0305 788255

Howletts Zoo
Bekesbourne
Nr Canterbury
Kent
Tel.: 0227 721410

The Otter Trust
Earsham
Nr Bungay
Suffolk
Tel.: 0986 3470

Addresses of other places in your area should be obtainable from Yellow Pages (under 'Nature conservancies and wildlife parks') or through local conservation organizations.

Practical organization

Costume

These are just suggestions. Costume may be as simple or as elaborate as you wish.
Debbie James: shirt, trousers, sleeveless jacket, boots.
Rhino group leader: khaki outfit — trousers, shirt, hat, boots, bag.
Gorilla group leader: khaki or camouflage outfit, hat, boots.
Polar Bear group leader: padded jacket or anorak, thick trousers, scarf, warm hat, gloves, snow boots.
Dolphin group leader: tracksuit, plimsolls.
Group leaders for Part D and controversial characters: any suitable outfit or item of clothing.

Settings

- Screens or large pieces of corrugated card showing backgrounds to habitats: An English hedgerow, a rainforest, the savanna, the Arctic, an ocean.
- Reverse of screens showing background to design areas.

Artefacts, materials, and equipment

Most of these will be easily obtainable. Some can be improvised, others could be omitted.
Tape recordings of sound effects are available from, Mike McMillan, Bulmershe College, Reading University, (Tel.: 0734 663387).

Part A

- The will

Part B

Group 1

- litter: waste paper, polythene, bottle tops, etc.
- tin can.
- carrot.

- bird's nest.
- drawing of footprints.
- picture of fox with family.
- picture of dead fox (from RSPCA).
- wire snare.
- tangle of fishing line.
- lead weights and old hooks mounted on card.
- tape recording of British birdsong.

BADGER TRACKS

Group 2

- photographs of gorillas in wild (from *Gorillas in the Mist*).
- photographs of habitat destruction (from *State of the Ark*).
- snares.
- celery.
- maps.
- tape recording of rainforest sounds.

Group 3

- globe.
- torch.
- telescope (real or made out of cardboard tube).
- binoculars (real or made out of cardboard).
- compass.
- emergency food rations (raisins, etc.).
- chart showing food chain.
- photographs of oil tankers in Arctic (ice-breakers).
- photographs of polar bears.
- tape of Arctic sounds.

MAGPIES NEST

Group 4

- Monofilament gill-net (sample from net manufacturers: see Yellow Pages).
- fishing line.
- photographs of dolphins and birds in distress from pollution, fishing nets, etc. (see *State of the Ark*).
- chart showing food chain.
- oil.
- feathers.
- Swarfega.
- disposable gloves.
- paper towels.

Group 5

- water bottles (any plastic bottles).
- photographs of rhino, illustrating work of rescue operations (available from Zoo Check).
- ash.
- notebook.
- compass.
- walkie-talkie (small tape recorder with recording of message from rhino patrol).
- tape recording of savanna sounds.

Part D

- each group is supplied with a board on which to build a model.

- basic materials, e.g. plasticine, blutac, straws, cardboard, pipe cleaners, twigs of evergreens, etc.
- the group designing the bus have special requirements, such as slides, pictures of animals, etc. from magazines; paper, felt-pens.

Preliminary practical work

Materials
- corrugated card.
- paper, paint, scissors, adhesive, etc.

The children are divided into five groups: Rhino, Polar Bear, Otter, Dolphin, and Gorilla. They make name badges showing group animal and their own first name. Do not tell them what will happen in the programme. This is most important.

The children make settings. In the groups, they paint cardboard to represent habitats. On reverse sides, they paint backgrounds to design areas.

Lesson Plans

These are for the teacher who is working alone or with one colleague.

The lessons are based on the programme *Animal Watch* and constant reference should be made to the programme when planning the lessons.

Some costume should be used for the roles (see suggestions for the programme).

Lesson 1
Preliminary practical work: As in programme.

Lesson 2
Role of teacher: Debbie James.

Extra artefacts:
- Any objects made out of animal or animal skin (rhino-foot umbrella stand, zebra-skin handbag, etc. — whatever you can find).
- Portfolio of pictures of animals in their natural habitats, especially otters, polar bears, gorillas, rhinos, elephants, dolphins.
- Pictures of animals in distress: snared otters, animals in small cages, polar bears in concrete pools (from Zoo Check).

Scenario: Debbie introduces herself as a country park ranger. She talks about her grandmother's travels, shows photographs of animals in the wild.

She explains her grandmother's concern that some animals are in danger of becoming extinct. Illustrates using pictures and objects. Finds out what the children feel about these animals.

She explains that her grandmother has left money in her will to help animals.

Debbie would like the children to help her to decide what to do with the money.

She is sending the children to various habitats to find out about different animals and their problems and needs. The children will then be asked to make a design for a way of using the legacy to benefit the animals which they have studied.

The next five lessons are in two parts and follow the group work in the programme. Part (a) is based on one of the habitats, part (b) on one of the design sections. During part (b), the teacher should change role to become a controversial character, as in the programme. In Lesson 3, this character could suggest the introduction of performing dolphins.

Costumes, settings, and artefacts: As for programme.

Lesson 3
Role of teacher: Marine biologist/conservationist.

PART (a) Base on Ocean habitat (Part B Group 4).

PART (b) Design a maritime centre which would be educational and beneficial to animals. It would be open to the public, so that visitors could learn about the ocean through displays, films, direct observation, etc.).

Issues:
- Pollution (rubbish, oil, industrial).
- Fishing (over-fishing, gill-nets, and danger to other creatures: dolphins, seabirds, small oceanic life, etc.).

Lesson 4
Role of teacher: Arctic researcher.
PART (a) Base on Arctic habitat (Part B, Group 3).
PART (b) Design improvements for an established zoo, especially to benefit Arctic animals, as in Part D.

Lesson 5
Role of teacher: Country Ranger.
PART (a) Base on English countryside habitat (Part B, Group 1).
PART (b) Design a country park, including an otter haven, as in Part D.

Lesson 6
Role of teacher: Gorilla researcher.
PART (a) Base on Rainforest habitat (Part B, Group 2).
PART (b) Design a gorilla sanctuary for saving breeding gorillas and, if possible, returning them to the wild (as in Part D).

Lesson 7
Role of teacher: Member of rhino-saving team, 'Operation Stronghold'.
PART (a) Base on Savanna habitat (Part B, Group 5).
PART (b) Design an educational bus for the Save the Rhino Campaign, as in Part D.

Lesson 8
Role of teacher: Debbie James.
Base lesson on Part E.
Finish off with discussion, as in Part F, with teacher out of role.

Follow-up work
As for programme.

The Learning Through Action Diploma Course

This one year, full-time course is the only qualification of its kind available in the country and is awarded by the University of Reading.

The course is intended for all teachers who believe in encouraging active learning across the curriculum and specifically for those who have an interest in the techniques of role-play. A candidate should be a serving teacher in an infant, junior, secondary or special school and should normally have a minimum of five years teaching experience.

Selection of course members depends on the candidates abilities to communicate with children and adults and to relate to their colleagues. It does not matter if teachers lack innate acting ability, since role-playing techniques are studied during the course. Candidates must be totally committed to the intentions of the course and should have the support and encouragement of the headteacher of their present school. The course requires that the methods that have been learned should be put into use on the teachers' return to school.

Further details of the course may be obtained from
The Learning Through Action Centre
Cumberland Road
Reading
Berks RG1 3JY
Tel: 0734 665556

CURRICULUM EXTENSION with LEARNING THROUGH ACTION

SEASONS OF CHANGE ages 8-13

Get your pupils really involved in history by offering them the opportunity to trace the history of farming for themselves. Information, pictures and prime source material allow them to explore the development of agriculture from the first farmers through Celts, Romans, Anglo-Saxons, and Normans to the 19th Century. By examining all aspects of farming life, from housing, clothing, and cooking to farming methods, pupils will build a solid base of knowledge and understanding from which to look at the issues facing agriculture and our countryside today.

Seasons of Change: £6.95

INUIT ages 8-13

What is it like to live in a community with no chief, no stealing, no word for war but 70 different words to describe snow? The Inuit pack will stimulate your pupils' interest and give them the opportunity to re-examine their own cultural values by looking at another very different lifestyle. In a topic pack which will create a term's work you will find details about the geography and history of the Inuit; the animals and plans that surround them; their hunting techniques; their clothes and dwelling places; their religion, family life, arts and crafts; their language and education. Finally, role play lessons examine the effect of Western civilization on the Inuit and seek to find solutions to their problems — and ours!

Inuit: £6.95

YANOMAMI ages 8-13

Using diaries and biographies of the Yanomami people, your pupils will discover the problems facing a people whose lifestyle is threatened with extinction because of the pursuit by others of minerals under the Amazon Rain Forest. Sex roles, the environment, health and hygiene, and many other aspects of this fascinating culture, give pupils the opportunity to explore issues and problems which have parallels in their own society.

Yanomani: £6.95

YOU ARE WHAT YOU EAT ages 5-8

What happens to the food we eat? This information pack, including story and work sheets, lets your pupils discover which foods are good for them and which should be eaten in moderation.

You are what you eat £5.50

WASTE NOT, WANT NOT ages 5-8
The story of Ben and his friends and how they make a wild-life garden in their city school. A teachers' pack gives background details and also information on recycling rubbish.

Waste Not, Want Not £5.50

ANIMAL WATCH ages 5-8
All the background information you need plus a set of work cards on animals and their habitats. Should animals be kept in captivity? How can endangered species be saved?

Animal Watch £8.50

MY LAND ages 8-13
The rich and eventful history of the Aborigines provides original and stimulating topic work with a wealth of opportunities for learning. By looking at the aboriginal language, their animals and plants, fishing and hunting, tools and weapons, trade and ceremony, art and craft, magic, music, and medicine, your pupils will learn what it is like to grow up as an Aborigine, and gain a real understanding of their complex and difficult history.

LD838 My Land £9.95

Available from LDA only

ISLANDS AT SEA ages 8-13
The newest addition to the Learning Through Action range, 'Islands at Sea' deals powerfully with life in the South Pacific today. Pupils are captivated by the nations of Fiji, Samoa, Soloman Islands, Tonga and the Marshall Islands.

By getting pupils to take the role of journalists, Islands at Sea gets them actively involved in finding out about different cultures. Once they've started they'll want to know more, and whether they are explaining the island's problems to visiting conservationists, making recordings of traditional dance music, or compiling the South Pacific newspaper, your pupils will be learning through action and enjoying it.

Islands at Sea gives you ten complete lesson plans plus a wealth of pupil material.

"A sensitively researched pack, giving economic and geographical background details with many ideas for classroom development. Even the slowest children become caught up in the energy and drama of the Islanders' lives."

Victoria Neumark
Times Educational
Supplement

Islands at Sea £6.95

TIME FOR CHANGE ages 8-13
Resource pack and lesson plans giving the background details of an Alkali factory in Widnes in 1850 to illustrate the pollution problems brought about by the Industrial Revolution. Of course, things are so much better today, aren't they? Your pupils will investigate modern pollution and possible solutions. A thought provoking and topical pack.

Time For Change £5.50

Please order from:

Learning Through Action Centre,
Cumberland Road,
READING
RG1 3JY
Berkshire
England
Tel: 0734 665556